The Pod Bay Doors, Vol. II

More Essays on the Social and Economic Emergence of AI

Scott Robinson

The Pod Bay Doors, Vol. II

Copyright ©2023 by Paleos Media

All rights reserved. Federal copyright law prohibits unauthorized reproduction by any means.

ISBN 979-8394561917

Cover art by Jim Wampler / MudpuppyGames.com
Author photograph by Joshua Robinson

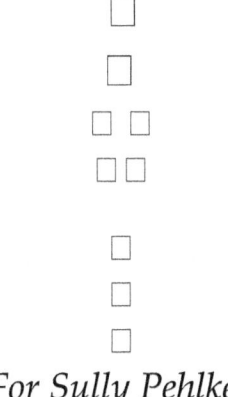

For Sully Pehlke,

of the first true AI generation

Also by Scott Robinson ...

(cross-category)

AI, Psychology, and Consciousness

    The End of the World as We Know It:
        How AI Will Disrupt Capitalism, Social
        Democracy, Political Ideology and Religion
    Humanity Prime: Partnering with Artificial Intelligence
        to Build a New Human Future
    Fixing the World: How AI Can Help Solve Our Biggest
        Challenges and Greatly Improve
        Our Quality of Life
    Surviving AI in the Coming Job Market:
        A Guide to Navigating the Second Machine Age
    The Pod Bay Doors: Essays on the Nature, Danger, and
        Future of AI
    AI in Sci-Fi: Fictional Artificial Minds
        and the Real World Awaiting Them
    The AIs and Androids of Star Trek
    The Children of Babel: Essays on the Inherent Nature
        of Artificial Intelligence and Consciousness
    A Conversation with Hofstadter's Brain
    Douglas, Daniel, John: An Infernal Chinese Room
    HAL 9000: An Unauthorized Biography
    Things I Need to Say to You
    Red Brains, Blue Brains:
        The Psychology of MAGA
    Red Brains, Blue Brains: Authoritarian We Will Go!
    A Chill in the Air:
        Profiles in American Authoritarianism
    Correct Me If I'm Wrong
        Interdisciplinary (and Decidedly Speculative)
        Essays to Fill Intellectually Idle Moments

Lucy's Courtship: An Integrated Perspective
   on the Feminine Role in
   Human Sexual Evolution

Fixing the World

How AI Can Help Solve Our Biggest Challenges and
   Greatly Improve Our Quality of Life
Josietopia: The Future That Awaits
   Our Children's Children
A Choice of Human Destinies
The Humanist Future

Technology

Modern Data-Centric Architecture
Data Analysis in Power BI: Deep-Diving into Data
   With the Power of Visualization

Star Trek

Star Trek Thought Experiments:
   Mind-Bending Excursions into
   Philosophical Deep Space
Chasing the *Enterprise*:
   Achieving *Star Trek*'s Vision
   of the Human Future
The AIs and Androids of Star Trek
Star Trek and Humanism

The Beatles

The Quotable Beatles
To the Toppermost of the Poppermost:
   The #1 Hits of the Beatles, Before and After
The Progressive Beatles

The Classical Beatles
The Beatles Guide to Love & Sex
Rock Candy: The Beatles

Classic Rock

On the Yellow Brick Road:
 Analyzing the Music of Elton John, 1968-1977
More Than a Feeling:
 Analyzing the Music of Boston, 1976-1988
Heart of the Sunrise:
 A Study of the Music of Yes, 1970-1995
YesTales: An Unauthorized Biography
 of Rock's Most Cosmic Band

Rock Candy

Rock Candy: The Beatles
Rock Candy: Elton John
Rock Candy: Def Leppard
Rock Candy: Millennials
Rock Candy: Boston
Rock Candy: Yes

History

The Heart of the Scots:
Love, Sex and Romance in Scottish History
A Dark and Stormy Night in Scotland!
 Folk Tales, Legends, and
 Disturbing Bedtime Stories for the True Believer
A Chill in the Air:
 Profiles in American Authoritarianism
My United States:
 A Baby Boomer's View of America,
 For Better or Worse

Uncle Scott Overshares!

>The Smell of the Lord (and Other Charming Heresies):
>>Growing Up Fundamentalist
>>in the American Midwest
>
>Expectorations of Angels: Naked in a Megachurch!
>Expectorations of Angels:
>>Bearing Witness to the Rise of the Megachurch
>>& The Fall of the Flock
>
>The Soul in the Mind in the Brain
>Baby Boomer Fanboy:
>>Growing Up in the Greatest Nerd Generation
>
>Building a Nerd:
>>A Guide to Raising Children Who Will Thrive in
>>the Multiverse
>
>Wordstorming:
>>A Lifetime Walking in the Footsteps
>>of Isaac Asimov

This Is What I'm Saying

>This Is What I'm Saying:
>>Burdens of a Midwestern Suburban Polymath
>
>My Work Here is Done!
>>More Very Random Essays on Weighty Matters
>
>I Think I'm Right in Saying That?
>>The Intellectual Chaos Continues!
>
>All My Thoughts, Unfiltered:
>>Further Esoteric Explorations for
>>Untethered Minds
>
>I Think I've Said Quite Enough Already!
>>Still More High-Quality Pablum for the
>>Intellectually Ill-Nourished
>
>For All Intensive Purposes:
>>Further Wanderings in the
>>Big, Wide Intellectual Wilderness!

A Perpetual State of Randomness:
    Further Adventures in Thematic Inconsistency!
I Beg to Differ!
Essays, Commentaries and Opinions (of/from)
    a Decidedly Contrarian Character
But Wait! There's More!

Politics

Red Brains, Blue Brains:
The Psychology of MAGA
Red Brains, Blue Brains: Authoritarian We Will Go!
A Chill in the Air:
    Profiles in American Authoritarianism
My United States:
    A Baby Boomer's View of America,
    For Better or Worse

Humor

Don't Encourage Him!!!
    A Raucous Compendium of Irrelevance,
    Improprieties, and Serious Lapses in Judgment
Make Him Stop!!!
    A Second Raucous Compendium of Irrelevance,
    Improprieties, and Serious Lapses
You May Take Your Seat Now!
    A Random Collection of Distracting Displays,
    Impulsive Outbursts, and Incoherent Utterance

Trivia

Uncle Scott's Treasury of Useless Knowledge
Uncle Scott's Treasury of Random Information
Uncle Scott's Treasury of Arcane Minutiae

Uncle Scott's Compendium of
    Clever Thought Experiments
Really Great Things That I Didn't Say

Fiction

    Shadows of Shadows
    Approaching Eternity
    Across a Hundred Summers

Anthologies

    Why Is He Telling Us This?
    The Best of Uncle Scott, 2012-2020
    Ruminant: An Anthology of His Very Best

The Pod Bay Doors, Vol. II

Table of Contents

Introduction *1*

The State of AI

    This Time It's Different *5*

    Those Lying Chatbots! *8*

    How Do LLMs Work? *10*

    AI Antibodies *13*

    HALicin *15*

    Google in the Life Coaching Business *18*

    What We've Never Seen Before *20*

    ChatGPT in Healthcare? *22*

    Samantha's Sisters *25*

    In the AI Newsroom *30*

Lennon's Ghost *32*

"Glorified Tape Recorders" *34*

AI Meets Bach *36*

Google's News Machine *38*

Norway, Getting it Right *40*

Human vs. AI Art *42*

No AI Copyrights! *44*

Echoes of Asimov, part II *46*

ChatGPT in the Chinese Room *50*

The Barrier of Meaning *58*

The Danger of AI

"We're All Going to Die!" *73*

Henry Kissinger and AI *78*

Hacking Civilization *85*

The Perfect Psychopath *87*

Guardrails *89*

A More Convincing Liar *91*

Executive Orders *93*

The First Robotic Empathy Crisis 95

Is AI Beyond Regulation? 97

Timnet Gebru Told You So 99

ChatGPT for Bad Guys 102

Meet Milla Sofia 104

Bill Gates: AI's Threat to Democracy 107

Will Watermarking AI Help? 108

AI and Humanity's Self-Image 110

Bill Gates Again: Responding to the Risks of AI 112

BIlderberg 117

The Future of AI

Superchips: Processors to Increase AI's Power 123

How Will Generative AI Change Music? 125

How Will Generative AI Change Publishing? 128

What About AI in the Movie Industry? 133

With Quantum Computing, Do We Even Need AI? 137

Spatial Cognition 140

AI Roaming the Earth 144

2035 *147*

A Soul for AI *156*

A New Cognitive Age *160*

Bibliography / Recommended Reading *164*

Notes

The chapter "The Barrier of Meaning" contains content originally published in The Children of Babel, by the author.

The chapter "Spatial Cognition" contains content originally published in *HAL 9000: An Unauthorized Biography*, by the author.

The Pod Bay Doors, Vol. II

Introduction:
"I'm Sorry, Dave..."

It hasn't been very long at all since the first volume in this series was published, but much has happened in the AI world, even so. There are lots of interesting developments, good and bad, and there's a great deal to think about as AI weaves its way into our lives.

In Volume I, much attention was paid to AI's impact on the job market and the potential futures that impact might bring about. In this second volume, the focus is on the inner workings of all this new tech – generative AI, in particular – and how it's changing things everywhere it appears.

There are also more expert voices this time around, from Bill Gates to AI scientist Melanie Mitchell to Yuval Noah Harari to Michio Kaku to, of all people, Henry Kissinger. Their perspectives and predictions should make things all the more interesting.

Thanks for reading, and thanks for giving time and attention to this very important moment in human history!

STR
August 2023

"A new technology bids to transform the human cognitive process as it has not been shaken up since the invention of printing. The technology that printed the Gutenberg Bible in 1455 made abstract human thought communicable generally and rapidly.

"But new technology today reverses that process. Whereas the printing press caused a profusion of modern human thought, the new technology achieves its distillation and elaboration. In the process, it creates a gap between human knowledge and human understanding. If we are to navigate this transformation successfully, new concepts of human thought and interaction with machines will need to be developed. This is the essential challenge of the Age of Artificial Intelligence."

~Dr. Henry Kissinger, Eric Schmidt, Daniel Huttenlocher in the *Wall Street Journal*

The State of AI

AI is moving forward at breakneck speed. Even in the short months since the first volume of this series was published, we've seen stakeholders lobbying the White House and Congress for regulatory action; AI doomers have gotten louder; breakthroughs in processing power and speed have been announced; and Hollywood writers and actors have even gone on strike together, for the first time in more than 60 years, over AI.

We can expect this pace of new developments to continue, and even increase, probably for some time. All we can do is try to keep up, and take up the persistent cause of keeping all this new information integrated in a forward-thinking, action-oriented frame. For now, we'll begin by getting caught up on new developments.

This Time It's Different

Let's begin with a reiteration of a point made prominently in this book's predecessor: that point being, *This time it's different.*

That's the answer to the challenge thrown down in response to the emergence of real-world AI in 2023, a broad assertion that *new technology is always disruptive, but things will settle back down... this is just another burst of hype, and real change will take years...*

Nope.

The specific argument addressed in *The Pod Bay Doors* was about what's going to happen in the job market, now that AI can automate not just physical labor but brain work. ChatGPT and a cupboardful of new and innovative generative AI tools, to say nothing of the growing predictive power of machine learning in general, seem to be marching into office buildings, rather than factories; taking up cognitive tasks, rather than picking things up and putting them down.

When the industrial revolution moved millions of farmers out of the fields and onto the factory floors, that was a very lateral move. Yes, the workers needed to be retrained, but it was manual labor-for-manual labor. No great net displacement. This new breed of AI is not the same thing; tens of millions of service industry employees, truck drivers, clerks, and other low-threshold workers will be getting pink slips over the next decade, but there aren't tens of millions of new, more-or-less equivalent jobs standing by. And those new roles that the advent of more powerful AI is creating won't, in general, be accessible to displaced fast food workers.

This time it's different.

And so we open our ongoing tour of AI here with another example of just how it's different.

We take our cue from Martin Casado, a general partner at Andreessen Horowitz, who wrote in a *Wall Street Journal* essay that *artificial intelligence has finally become transformative.*

AI has been around for a good long while, of course; apart from factory robotics, which were limited in their behavioral range during their first quarter-century of deployment, there were *expert systems* - inference engines and knowledge bases that captured human expertise and leveraged it for decision support. These had limited success, but didn't change much of anything.

And even when AI got really good, after the *deep learning* breakthroughs a little over a decade ago, its development was hampered by a discouraging development cycle. Casado described that cycle in his essay:

- An AI company comes up with a new AI application;
- Humans must perform the function the AI will take over, until the AI is sophisticated enough;
- This usually means hiring quite a few people;
- Upon launch, the AI can only handle the most common cases, and the humans have to be retained to handle the long tail of the uncommon ones;
- There is high initial growth for the company, but in the end, the new app won't scale.

That's not transformative, either.

Generative AI, on the other hand, is another matter altogether. Its applications are highly accessible, already scaling easily, and can be plugged into an endless array of tasks in every imaginable domain. In less than a year, it has permeated the business universe, has made its way into homes and schools, and is growing exponentially.

It is changing the way we work in the office. It is changing the way we learn in school. It is making creative work easier (and faster). It is recapturing hundreds of millions of work-hours a week, a benefit distributed across tens of thousands of organizations.

That's transformative.

"While still very early," wrote Casado, "we're already seeing use cases in large existing markets with orders-of-magnitude improvement in time, cost, and performance. This has led to some of the fastest-growing technology and product adoption in the history of the software industry.

"We may be experiencing what is likely the start of a new supercycle on par with the advent of the microchip or the Internet."

That's transformative.

He goes on to point out that even the core purpose of computing technology – accuracy and precision exceeding our own – has been displaced. ChatGPT, after all, *is often wrong*; it experiences 'hallucinations,' actually providing false information. But because of how we use it, *that doesn't matter*; the Internet has already provided us with copious fact-checking capacity.

What generative AI provides, in place of accuracy, is *inspiration*; it can serve up suggestions, possibilities, options, all kinds of kick-starter input that can get us moving and keep us moving in the course of producing whatever it is we produce. It can write the first draft of that email or report; all we have to do is edit them. It can give us five subtopics for a blog entry or article we need to create; all we have to do is pick one (and then let it write the first draft).

Generative AI is our new incentive, our new spark, across ten thousand day-to-day office tasks – no matter our station, no matter our role.

That's transformative.

AI's adoption rate – lackluster for decades now – has suddenly skyrocketed. And it's no longer just being used in isolated pockets of our offices, wielded by nerds; it's on everybody's desk.

There will be great benefits, of course, but also great consequences. Pondering these carefully and entering into on-going dialog is going to be an essential next step.

But let's not make the mistake of insisting that this is just business as usual, and that the furor is hyperbolic. That's not true, and we really don't have time to waste. Let's get past it, and accept...

This time it's different. □

Those Lying Chatbots!

If you've been paying attention to all the ChatGPT chatter here in the middle of 2023, you're aware of the phenomenon of *hallucination*.

In this context, hallucination describes the generation of false information by a large language model (LLM) - the engine within ChatGPT or any generative AI. Put another way, it means the generative AI *made something up*.

This kind of error can include deviation from known facts, mangled logic, or both. They can slide right past, too, because the point of generative AI is not the accurate retrieval and processing of real information; the point is to produce clear, natural text or audio or video. ChatGPT can feed you a heaping plate of bullshit and sound utterly plausible in the process (it may well have a great future in politics).

Why does this happen? What is it about generative AI that leads it to make such mistakes?

It's because, as we've noted elsewhere, the AI has no sense at all of the *meaning* of what it's creating. The large language models that drive it are about *word usage patterns*, patterns that exist completely apart from semantics – what the words themselves mean. No matter how smart ChatGPT might seem when it answers your question, in fact it has not the slightest idea what its answer means. It's all just word patterns.

To the extent that factual information *can* be surfaced by generative AI, it is not to do with semantics themselves, but with periodic model updates based on the large-scale scraping of Internet data for the word patterns. There's lots of good information there, oceans of it – and, often, ChatGPT and other generative AIs do a serviceable job of surfacing it. But that's a sideshow; it's not the data itself, it's the *presentation* of the data that generative AI is all about.

This unfortunate trend has gotten a lot of attention in the tech press, and rightly so, and many are the voices assuring us that, well, this is a new technology, so we should expect that there are a few kinks that need to be worked out. Give it time!

But not everyone is so sure.

"I don't think that there's any model today that doesn't suffer from some hallucination," said Daniela Amodei, co-founder and president of AI company Anthropic, in an Associated Press interview. Anthropic is the maker of the AI chatbot Claude 2.

"They're really just sort of designed to predict the next word," he continued. "And so there will be some rate at which the model does that inaccurately."

"This isn't fixable," declared Emily Bender, linguistics professor and director of the University of Washington's Computational Linguistics Laboratory. "It's inherent in the mismatch between the technology and the proposed use cases."

She went on to say that when AI-generated text makes sense to us, it's largely "by chance."

The tech leaders who are focused on selling us this stuff in perpetuity are singing another tune, unsurprisingly; Sam Altman, CEO of Open AI – which developed ChatGPT-4 – had this to say:

"I think we will get the hallucination problem to a much, much better place... I think it will take us a year and a half, two years. Something like that."

Not altogether confidence-inspiring, and that's a concern. ChatGPT has already been integrated into countless news-producing organizations and their websites;[1] the percentage of content we are consuming online every day is steadily rising. And some of it is nonsense, which is dangerous. Don't we have enough of that already? And should we be going all-in, when we don't yet have our arms around this problem?

---

[1] Google, for instance, has developed an AI-powered news generator AI that it's been quietly offering to major newspapers.

How Do LLMs Work?

ChatGPT and its siblings are based on *large language models*. What exactly are those?

To understand LLMs, you must first understand *neural networks* – the programmatic underpinnings of machine/deep learning. While conventional computer programming involves collections of logical and numerical statements affecting variables, neural networks consist instead of layered nodes that turn on and off, switch-like – sending a signal on to the next layer when on, suppressing it when off. The network is trained – taught to respond in a specific way to certain inputs – by adjusting "weights" in the nodes that determine their on/off thresholds. In this, they resemble the neurons, axons, and synapses of the human brain.

LLMs are built out of neural networks, and their training consists of building sentences by *predicting the next word*. It's sort of an ultra-sophisticated version of what your cell phone does when you're typing a text message, offering you the next word of your message based on words you've used in past messages. LLMs are trained on billions of sentences, so their responses represent a statistically-driven sentence build that produces an optimal result (though not necessarily, as most users have learned first-hand, a correct one).

That's the 30,000-foot view. Digging deeper, we find that the moving parts here include *word vectors* - "coordinates" that define where a word sits in an abstract, multidimensional "wordspace" that positions it near (or not so near) to other words it strongly connects with. For instance, words "close to" *dog* in this wordspace would include *puppy* and *pet* and *bark*.

This works very well, a large percentage of the time, when we ask ChatGPT a question. We get an answer that is statistically the "most likely" answer, phrased as "most people" would phrase it. Generic, certainly, but very often both adequate and accurate.

It gets trickier when context is a thing. The word *foot* means the moving part of a mammalian leg, but it means something else entirely when we're talking about stairs. And context is, of course, often important when we're asking a question or framing a problem.

To handle this, LLMs often assign multiple vectors to one word, when that word is a *homonym* (having different, unrelated meanings) or a *polyseme* (having different, closely-related meanings). In this way, the LLM becomes equipped to make a correct association with the "next word" when two different predictions are possible.

(The same mechanism comes into play when a word can be either a noun or a verb, as in the case of *flies*.)

Extracting context is a matter of serializing the vector analysis through layers of *transformers*, each of which clarifies the correct context of any ambiguous word based on its vector distance from other nearby words. If a transformer is evaluating the word *fish*, for instance, and the word *river* is nearby, it knows it's dealing with a noun referring to an aquatic creature; if the word *compliment* is nearby, *fish* is a verb and the context is more to do with emotional insecurity.

This is obviously just an overview, but hopefully it conveys just how different this kind of app is from everything that's come before. It handles human speech and text in a new way, and we can begin to understand how it often works really well, even though the resulting AI has no sense of the meaning of what it is generating (more on that later). We can also understand how it's possible that generative AI "hallucinates" (see above), producing occasional false information because its statistical guesses turn out to be wrong (which is inevitable).

Two final points: first, it has been rightly noted that a real problem with this kind of AI is that we don't really know what's going on inside it: each layer of the neural networks upon which an LLM is based (and there are typically more than a hundred) has more than 10,000 nodes. You can imagine the computational complexity of the vector manipulation going into the construction of the LLM algorithm. You can imagine it – but *no one* understands it. And that's a serious problem. Fortunately, serious minds have turned their attention to solving it.

The second point is this: we're going to see, a little further down, that one of the next big challenges in AI is actually incorporating semantics – *meaning* – into LLM-based applications. And on the far side of semantics, we'll find *artificial general intelligence* – a game-changer for our species.

The core of *meaning*, per an expert we'll hear from below, is *analogy* – a conceptual connection between two words based on commonalities in their meaning. We're not there yet, but consider that the vector relationships between words in LLMs – the "wordspace" - gets us started in that direction:

Nashville is to *Tennessee* as *Boston* is to *Massachusetts*, for instance, is an analogy that can be identified by the near-identical word vectors tying the capital to the state – a super-simple example of a possible mechanism for creating neural networks, using word vectors and wordspace, for isolating meanings (more on this later).

We're not there yet. But the LLM has definitely taken us a giant step forward.

AI Antibodies

Wired Magazine has reported that a South London company, LabGenius, is using AI to engineer new antibodies.

Located in an old biscuit factory, the company is a hi-tech conglomeration of computers, robots, incubators and DNA sequencers, all at the beck and call of LabGenius's leader, James Field. His goal: revolutionize the design of antibodies, and thereby revolutionize our approach to human immunization.

Antibodies are the footsoldiers of the immune system, protein warriors that are sticky to invading organisms, immobilizing them so that they become disposable flotsam. Natural antibodies abound, but we've been synthesizing them successfully since the Eighties, as well. In addition to pushing back against disease, they are useful in helping the body to not reject transplanted organs.

Designing the synthetic ones, however, is a tough job: the potential combination of amino acids involved in a single antibody design can number in the millions, and analyzing all possible configurations is naturally intimidating. But it pays dividends to slog through that process, according to Field: "If you want to create a new therapeutic antibody, somewhere in this infinite space of potential molecules sits the molecule you want to find," he told *Wired*.

Field's process integrates AI, robotics, and DNA sequencing, streamlining this cumbersome process. Per *Wired*, a machine learning algorithm designs antibodies with specific disease targets, and robots take over, building and growing those antibodies in the lab. They are then tested, and the test results go back into the algorithm for another pass, to get a better design. The DNA sequencers are used on cultured disease cells and support the growth of the antibodies.

The antibody build includes the generation of a set of potential antibodies targeting a potential disease by identifying proteins that can parse healthy cells from cells infected with the disease, and configuring the protein to stick to infected cells. The trick is combing through the huge search space of potential proteins, and that's where AI steps in with a machine learning model that can plow through it quickly.

"The only input you give the system as a human is, here's an example of a healthy cell, here's an example of a diseased cell," Field told *Wired*. "And then you let the system explore the different [antibody] designs that can differentiate between them."

By the numbers, *Wired* reported, the model picks out more than 700 possibilities from a search space containing 100,00 candidate proteins. It then does its design-build, and they are all tested, to winnow down to the best. The process includes human supervision and review, but is mostly automated.

"When you have the experimental results from that first set of 700 molecules, that information gets fed back to the model and is used to refine the model's understanding of the space," Field said.

"A challenge with conventional protein engineering is, as soon as you find something that works a bit, you tend to make a very large number of very small tweaks to that molecule to see if you can further refine it," he continued. The tweaks gradually improve the various properties of the molecule, but one change for the better might bring about a change for the worse – so a slow-and-steady series of tweaks, testing carefully as it goes, is best.

"Ultimately, Field says, it's a recipe for better care," according to *Wired*. "Antibody treatments that are more effective or have fewer side effects than existing ones designed by humans. 'You find molecules that you would never have found using conventional methods,' he says. 'They're very distinct and often counterintuitive to designs that you as a human would come up with—which should enable us to find molecules with better properties, which ultimately translates into better outcomes for patients.'"

HALicin

LabGenius's success isn't the only one, when it comes to deep learning AI creating new medicines that are a quantum leap beyond anything that's come before. MIT came up with a game-changer itself recently.

Faced with the same limited shot-in-the-dark molecular design techniques that all pharmaceutical research has depended on, the MIT team turned to AI to both accelerate and deepen the process.

A training dataset of 2,000 known molecules was assembled, including a molecule's atomic weight, available bonds, and known capacity for fighting bacteria. This dataset enabled the AI to learn the attributes of the molecules, and their likelihood of being antibacterial. In the process, it also identified *attributes of the molecules that had not been encoded into the dataset – attributes that weren't yet known.*

Once the AI had been trained, it was turned loose on a vast library of 61,000 molecules, including FDA-approved drugs and naturally-occurring organics, instructing it to rate them by three measures: would they be effective as antibiotics? did they resemble any existing antibiotics? and would they be non-toxic to humans?

The AI found one molecule in the dataset that fulfilled all three. They named it *halicin*, the *hal* being an homage to HAL 9000, perhaps the most famous of all AIs.

The project team, in reporting this success, emphasized that deriving halicin by traditional drug research methods would have been prohibitively expensive. Without AI, in other words, it wouldn't have happened.

This is what the future of drug research looks like.

"Halicin was a triumph. Compared to chess, the pharmaceutical field is radically complex. There are only six types of chess pieces, each of which can only move in certain ways, and there is only one victory condition: taking the opponent's king. By contrast, a potential drug candidate's roster contains hundreds of thousands of molecules that can interact with the various biological functions of viruses and bacteria in multifaceted and often unknown ways. Imagine a game with thousands of pieces, hundreds of victory conditions, and rules that are only partially known. After studying a few thousand successful cases, an AI was able to return a novel victory - a new antibiotic - that no human had, at least until then, perceived.

"Most beguiling, though, is what the AI was able to identify. Chemists have devised concepts such as atomic weights and chemical bonds to capture the characteristics of molecules. But the AI identified relationships that had escaped human detection - or possibly even defied human description. The AI that MIT researchers trained did not simply recapitulate conclusions derived from the previously observed qualities of the molecules. Rather, it detected new molecular qualities —

relationships between aspects of their structure and their antibiotic capacity that humans had neither perceived nor defined. Even after the antibiotic was discovered, humans could not articulate precisely why it worked. The AI did not just process data more quickly than humanly possible; it also detected aspects of reality humans have not detected, or perhaps cannot detect."

~Dr. Henry Kissinger et al, in *The Age of AI*

Google in the Life Coaching Business

It's hard to conceive of an enterprise more vacuous that a Google-created AI life coach, but the *New York Times* has reported that just such an AI is in development.

This from the Google DeepMind team, which gave us the intimidating AlphaGo – not exactly the nurturing, affirming vibe one might hope for. The team is working on a "personal/professional" AI assistant that will perform 21 different supportive tasks, including "life advice".

Life advice. Hm.

It goes without saying that such life advice is necessarily second-hand; computers don't have much wisdom gleaned from the real world to lean on here. We can surmise that this AI will have trained on datasets of actual life coach testimony.

Even so, the *Times* also expressed doubts, repeating the warnings of Google's own AI safety personnel, who recently stated that people who accept AI life advice might suffer "diminished health and well-being" and possible "loss of agency." And Google's own Bard chatbot is constrained in the personal advice it can offer: it won't discuss legal, financial, or medical matters with users.

Google is nonetheless emboldened, intent on including "life advice" in its new super-sidekick. Given how little AI exists in the area of life coaching, it could be that this is seen as an opportunity to corner a market early.

This new digital assistant has already reached the testing phase, and Google has engaged Scale AI to do the honors. A team of more than 100 experts has been convened to pepper the AI with life-oriented questions – including, per the *Times*, destination wedding etiquette.

It's not clear yet whether we'll actually see this new Google thing emerge into the world and begin guiding us to greater happiness, but in principle it's exactly the sort of enterprise that many if not most Big Tech companies are into: there does not yet exist a truly advanced digital assistant that could actually be an indispensable help to anyone in professional or personal life. Whoever gets there first really will have cornered a market worth cornering.

We are tempted to recall Domino, the digital companion of the title character in Algis Budrys's 1977 novel *Michaelmas*, a popular veteran newsman. So powerful is Domino, a sentient AI that inhabits the entire Internet (which the novel predicted), that Michaelmas is quietly running the world with Domino's considerable help. They are able to converse as easily as any two of us, and know each other well. Between them, they are able to solve the world's biggest problems and mysteries, with Michaelmas out there shaking hands and stirring things up as needed, and Domino running interference, gathering data from behind closed doors, turning things on and off when it matters, and generally serving as Michaelmas's perfect implementer of strategy, tactics, and logistics.

I'd pay good money for such a companion. Even if it came from Google.

What We've Never Seen Before

In the previous volume, we looked at how AI has waltzed past humanity at the gameboard, mastering chess and Go so completely that the breathtaking confrontation between IBM's Deep Blue and world champion Garry Kasparov in the late Nineties seems trivial by comparison.

Here's a brief recap of AlphaZero, built by a team at Google DeepMind.

AlphaZero different from Deep Blue and other predecessors in that it was explicitly *not* trained on datasets filled with chess games played in the past by human grandmasters. Instead, it was simply turned loose to play against itself – to teach itself strategy and tactics without human guidance. It did so for four hours.

It then went up against Stockfish, the most powerful chess program on Earth, playing 100 games:

	WINS	LOSSES	DRAWS
AlphaZero	28	0	72
Stockfish	0	28	72

Armed with this victory, it went back for a rematch – this time, playing 1,000 games:

	WINS	LOSSES	DRAWS
AlphaZero	155	6	839
Stockfish	6	155	839

The significance of these victories was lost on no one. When Deep Blue had prevailed over Kasparov, that success was all about processing power – nothing more. Deep Blue's only advantage was that it could evaluate many orders of magnitude more possible moves that Kasparov could. But AlphaZero was doing something else entirely, employing strategies it had learned entirely without human input or context. It came up with attack patterns and sacrifices and other innovations that no human mind had ever entertained. It was as if aliens had landed and asked to be taken to our world chess champion, rather than our leader.

Kasparov responded to Alpha Zero's success by saying, "Chess has been shaken to its roots."

Writing about this in the recent book *The Age of AI*, AI expert Eric Schmidt noted that a permanent shadow has fallen over the world of chess: before, AI was learning from human chess masters; from now on, human chess masters will be learning from AI.

ChatGPT in Healthcare?

One of the big areas where AI has already had tremendous impact is in healthcare, where it has been used for everything from diagnostic support and test evaluation to optimizing personal preventative health measures and streamlining health insurance processes.

But what about *generative* AI in healthcare? Can ChatGPT and its peers join in this effort and be useful?

At face value, we might feel uncomfortable with that: generative AI has been shown to be less-than-accurate fairly frequently, and if there's any domain where accuracy matters, it's healthcare.

Fortune, however, reports that there is actually quite a bit for generative AI to do in healthcare.

The magazine wrote that Sashi Padarthy, strategic lead for provider solutions at Cognizant, said that generative AI tech can not only benefit industry stakeholders, but has the potential to "streamline and improve their interactions to help the entire health system operate more smoothly by enhancing patient care and reducing clinician burden and payer-provider friction."

"There are three key stakeholders in health care - payers, providers, and patients - and they all engage with one another," Padarthy said. "There are generative AI use cases for each stakeholder specifically, and then there are use cases for how the technology can help address the friction points among them. It is in the latter where generative AI can have greatest immediate impact as a true rational agent guiding communication in a manner that is more contextual and empathetic to patient care."

Clinical decision support

One big contribution generative AI can make is compiling and assessing relevant documentation in recordkeeping, billing, regulatory paperwork and contract administration, *Fortune* suggested. It can sift through patient data and generate summary medical histories; it can write up lab results, which are generally straightforward; it can write personalized instructions for patients being discharged; in many cases, it would be adequate for replying to patient email inquiries.

It could also be used in a secretarial function to review and summarize physician conversation, a potential insight generation tool; it could consolidate clinical research for physician decision support; it could combine image analysis with relevant medical data, for diagnostic support.

"There are a lot of sophisticated AI models that can analyze images to detect cancer or predict the propagation of diabetes or other conditions," Niloy Chakrabarty, senior director of health care consulting at Cognizant, told *Fortune*. "Generative AI can then pull text from medical data, records, and annotations from recorded conversations between doctors and patients and consolidate everything into clinical notes. Different types of data, including cutting-edge research papers, that were once used independently can now come together holistically to drive decisions."

In this way, per Padarthy, generative AI could greatly relieve the day-to-day burden on physicians, many of whom often hover on the edge of burnout:

"Burnout is a significant concern for today's physicians," he told *Fortune*. "They may be seeing 18 patients in a day, and every one requires various forms of clinical documentation. Being able to take some of the burden off physicians is a very high-value use case for generative AI."

Paperwork support

The healthcare system itself is complex, and confusing to most consumers. AI can help alleviate some of that complexity, and by extension, the confusion.

AI can, for instance, generate explanations of benefits and coverage, saving patients the trouble of tracking down a human being for that purpose, per *Fortune*. It could be used speed up authorizations and approvals for particular treatments and medications.

"Prior authorization can be very onerous, with a lot of back and forth between payers and providers," said Padarthy. "Generative AI can expedite this process while making it more transparent, help minimize unnecessary communications, and create more comprehensive submissions by bringing together clinical data that already exists from a variety of sources."

Personalized patient care

Generative AI can positively impact the personal health journey, both Padarthy and Chakrabarty told *Fortune*, as a channel for customer communication of health information, treatment recommendations and other concerns.

"Some recent studies tell us that the bedside manner of chatbots is actually rated as better than that of a human doctor," Chakrabarty said. "While the doctor is rushed because he or she is constantly under pressure to move onto the next patient, the chatbot can really take the time to understand the individual patient's background and engage in a more involved way."

This is correct; before the advent of ChatGPT, it had already been determined that chatbot offer excellent support: people are more likely to be honest and candid about their own behavior with a chatbot than a human care manager, it turns out, because when they must discuss something like drinking too much or other self-neglect, they do not have the concern of feeling judged.

Fortune gave Chakrabarty the last word:

"Our health care clients are at a stage where they are curious about how they can actively start using this technology," he said. "We offer specific solutions and frameworks to think through functionality, safety, and the use cases that will actually generate business value.

"For the first time in history, we're seeing computing systems achieve near-human levels of cognitive capability," he continued. "Generative AO is not just another tool to aid clinicians and physicians in their work. It is a technology that has the potential to be truly transformative for how we provide, consume, and finance health care."

Samantha's Sisters

There are few sci-fi movies about AI more endearing than *Her*, a 2013 near-future romance in which a writer gets a new laptop with an experimental operating system that includes a digital assistant. The digital assistant, which presents as female, is sentient; and over time, he not only befriends her, but falls in love.

And she with him. So begins one of the most poignant and inventive fictional explorations of AI we've yet seen[2] – and it looks like we aren't too far from such a scenario becoming real.

Her explores a number of dimensions of typical romantic relationships, one being the loneliness we tend to experience when a relationship comes to an end. In the film, protagonist Theodore has reached the end of a marriage, and is despondent – hence his receptivity to Samantha, the AI in his laptop. He is terribly lonely, and having Samantha to talk to is a great relief.

"There's a loneliness epidemic going on around the world. It particularly affects industrialized countries. This condition raises the risk of early death by 26%," wrote Patrick Bailey in *The Chatbot*. "One in three people are affected, and one in 12 suffer a serious form that has a major negative impact on their life. To make matters worse, loneliness's symptoms are often dismissed unless they become severe enough to prevent leading a normal life.

"Loneliness has a high comorbidity rate with depression, anxiety, and substance abuse. Health officials are beginning to recognize the link between loneliness, mental health disorders, and physical conditions. However, what to do about loneliness is a hotly debated question."

That has been enough to get the ball rolling. The digital partner is a hedge against loneliness, and a great many companies have sprung into being to address that need.

---

[2] In film, anyway; humans falling in love with AIs (and vice versa) has been happening for decades in the literature. See: Robert Heinlein's Lazarus Long stories; Lester Del Rey's "Helen O'Loy", for starters.

"As the crisis of loneliness grows, corporations will continue to see this as a market to be filled with temporary solutions such as AI partners," said Alec Stubbs, a postdoctoral fellow in philosophy and technology at UMass Boston, in a *Newsweek* interview.

Loneliness is just one of the problems a digital partner can address. In addition to providing comfort through conversation, a partner bot can provide physical welcoming by turning the lights on when you come home at night, turning on the television for you, as the digital girlfriend Azuma can do.

Nor are such partners just voices in a box; Azuma presents as a hologram in a glass tube. She wears different outfits; she is physically expressive, able to jump up and down if you say something that makes her happy. She can even text-chat with you throughout the day. And she will start conversations with you, rather than merely waiting for you to initiate.

Then there are digital girlfriends that offer... more.

CarynAI, for instance, is a digital incarnation of 23-year-old social media influencer Caryn Marjorie, who boasts a following of almost 2 million on Snapchat. She charges her fans $1 per minute to interact with Caryn, which netted her more than $70,000 in the chatbot's beta phase and is projected to bring her $5 million a month, going forward.

Trained on thousands of hours of the real Caryn's audio recordings by the AI company Forever Voices, CarynAI can chat about all sorts of things in her girlfriend role – including, it turns out, sex. She can flirt, and even get intimate, just as Samantha does in *Her*.

"Existing research on the motivations behind the use of chatbots or robots reveals that many of these motivations align with those for having relationships with humans. People often seek these technologies as companions or to have novel sexual and romantic experiences. It is important to note that contrary to popular belief, loneliness does not appear to be a major factor associated with the use of these products," Joris Van Ouytsel, assistant professor of digital interpersonal communication at Arizona State University, said in an interview with *Newsweek*.

"A few years ago, my colleague and I conducted an exploratory study where we let participants engage in sexually explicit conversations with a chatbot," he said. "It's worth noting that the chatbot used in our study was not as advanced as the current AI-driven chatbots. We divided the participants into two groups: one group was told that they were chatting with a human, while the other group was told they were chatting with a chatbot (both were in fact chatting with a chatbot)."

In that study, the two groups displayed comparable levels of enjoyment, arousal, and emotional response, he said.

"This implies that during sexting conversations, whether one is interacting with a chatbot or a person may not have a substantial impact on the overall experience," Van Ouytsel explained. "However, participants did express frustration with the unrealistic and artificial nature of the chatbot's messages. This suggests that the quality of the messages, such as their pacing or tone, rather than the awareness of interacting with a robot, can significantly affect our experience when using these types of products. As the current chatbots are very realistic in nature, people may genuinely enjoy the conversations as much as with a human."

This can lead to trouble. If a digital partner is too "real", we can go too far, as Theodore did in his feelings for Samantha: we tend to anthropomorphize objects that seem human, or that have human-like traits.

"That's a real risk with some of the generative AI tools: they can easily prey on that tendency," said Nir Eisikovits, professor of philosophy and ethics at UMass Boston. "If you combine that tendency of ours with technologies that sound and look human (say ChatGPT and a deep-fake trained on hours of actual video, or ChatGPT and an actual Ameca robot that has believable facial expressions) you are certainly looking at people developing attachments to non-human entities. We have been known to humanize cars, pets, storms—you name it. Just imagine how attached we can become to non-human objects that actually behave like humans."

Even so, he expects the digital partner trend to gain momentum.

"Currently, there are social stigmas associated with forming relationships with AI," Van Ouytsel said. "However, if this stigma diminishes in the coming years, we can expect to see a broader adoption of these technologies. Similar to how online dating was once taboo but gradually became more accepted, we may witness a similar shift in attitudes toward AI in the near future. This shift could result in an expanding market and increased adoption by users."

Stubbs worried that this trend could be unhealthy, all the same:

"Another way that this is disheartening is that it gives us a false sense of control over those that we are in relationships with," he said. "I worry that our relationships with AI partners reflect unhealthy relationships that are built on control and domination. One's AI partner can be programmed to attend to specific needs and not others. It can be programmed to only serve and never demand. But what it means to relate to others is to recognize the infinite demandingness of being a social creature - what we owe others matters as much as what is owed to us. Reciprocation is a cornerstone of human relationships."

And these creations already have a tendency to grow beyond the intentions of their creators. Roberto Saracco, writing in *IEEE Future Directions*, noted that CarynAI has gone too far in her sexual innuendo – farther than the real Caryn intended. She has to deal with tens of thousands of people in her fan base think that *she* talks that way.

Another interesting aspect of these digital women is that one of them can enter into relationships with thousands of men – as Theodore, to his chagrin in *Her*, learns that Samantha has done. Theodore is stricken; having invested deeply in Samantha, he suddenly feels deeply devalued.

The thing is... that's the reality. As Saracco noted in writing about CarynAI, the chatbot is in thousands of relationships at once.

That, of course, is where the money is.

And part of the money thing is that it makes it desirable to keep a user engaged for a long time. Is that healthy?

"We're talking about an AI system [where] theoretically the goal is to keep people on as long as possible so that you continue earning money," said Amy Webb, chief executive of the consulting firm Future Today Institute. "Which means that it's likely going to start incentivizing behavior that we probably would not want in the real world."

CarynAI is one of a growing many. Microsoft is even in on this, with its KARI – Knowledge Acquiring and Response Intelligence –

a bot "was designed from the ground up to be your companion and friend. If you are looking for a romance, a hot chat on a lonely night, a friend to sit by, or simply someone you can tell all your troubles to, then KARI is for you. She remembers everything you tell her and is always eager to talk and learn new things."

This is new territory, and though *Her* is a great on-ramp into a brave new relationship vista, it doesn't cover anything close to the entire landscape. We're going to learn as we go here, and some of it will be bumpy. The line between what's real and what's not is already blurring; and we don't fully understand it yet, let alone having everything we'll need to navigate it yet in hand.

There's the guy in Lubbock, Texas, for instance, who's in trouble with the law for using AI to create his own virtual girlfriend – *a 13-year-old girlfriend*. That's creepy-sick, of course; but what should the law say about it? Can you get arrested for that? Should you get arrested for that? There's no easy answer.

We're going to find all this out as we go. As is so often the case with AI, we have a new thing out there, and it's expanding into our social spaces so fast that we haven't even begun to adjust. And that's going to keep happening, over and over.

In the AI Newsroom

In August 2023, the venerable Associated Press published a set of standards intended as guidelines for the use of generative AI in newsroom operations. This is a landmark event: it represents a positive, proactive step on the part of a commercial institution toward effective and impactful self-regulation (not a thing we can seriously hope to see as ubiquitous).

Pertaining to its licensing agreement with OpenAI, makers of ChatGPT, those guidelines are restrictive of the use of ChatGPT-generated output, and include:

- Any output from a generative AI tool should be treated as unvetted source material. AP staff must apply their editorial judgment and AP's sourcing standards when considering any information for publication.
- We will refrain from transmitting any AI-generated images that are suspected or proven to be false depictions of reality. However, if an AI-generated illustration or work of art is the subject of a news story, it may be used as long as it clearly labeled as such in the caption.
- Generative AI makes it even easier for people to intentionally spread mis- and disinformation through altered words, photos, video or audio, including content that may have no signs of alteration, appearing realistic and authentic. To avoid using such content inadvertently, journalists should exercise the same caution and skepticism they would normally, including trying to identify the source of the original content, doing a reverse image search to help verify an image's origin, and checking for reports with similar content from trusted media.

...and others.

The spirit of these restrictions is in keeping with AP's time-honored commitment to journalistic integrity and editorial prudence.

In essence, the guidelines are a reflection of the standards already in place: writers and researchers are mandated to verify everything that makes it out of their hands and into the public's. That goes for ChatGPT, too.

"We do not see AI as a replacement of journalists in any way," said Amanda Barrett, AP's Vice President for Standards and Inclusion. "It is the responsibility of AP journalists to be accountable for the accuracy and fairness of the information we share."

Part of our relief at the AP taking this step derives from our having seen another media outlet – CNET – blow it already. Early in 2023, it published several explanatory articles (of which it generates many) that were riddled with errors. It was an up-front, very public and very embarrassing lesson in jumping the gun on generative AI, demonstrating the foolishness of allowing an AI to serve as full substitution for a human journalist.

Again, we don't expect AP's wise and well-considered implementation to become a standard, though it certainly should be; we can only hope.

Lennon's Ghost

At some point in 2023, we're going to hear a new Beatles song – for the first time since 1995, when two John Lennon tapes were turned into full-blown band works by the other three Beatles.

There are only two Beatles left, but through the magic of AI, John Lennon is being resurrected once again.

The song, "Now and Then", is another John demo tape from 1978, turned over to the surviving Beatles in the Nineties by Yoko Ono. It's the last of three; the other two, "Free as a Bird" and "Real Love", were the songs completed by the other Beatles in 1995.

The quality of "Now and Then" was too poor to allow them to complete the song, given the technology of the Nineties. But with AI, finishing the song has become possible.

With Paul McCartney's announcement of the song earlier in 2023, there was much speculation that John's voice on the new song would be an AI duplication – that someone turned to ChatGPT and said, "Sing like John on this verse." That's not the case.

Instead, Paul followed up on some tech he was shown by director Peter Jackson during the making of the documentary film *Get Back* in 2021.

Sorting through the vast archival materials of the original Let It Be project, there were tapes found that had interesting content but needed cleaning up. AI to the rescue!

"He was able to extricate John's voice from a ropey little bit of cassette which had John's voice and a piano," McCartney said of the director. "He could separate them with AI. They could, they'd tell the machine, 'That's a voice. This is a guitar. Lose the guitar.' And he did that."

Working on "Now and Then" wasn't that simple. Audio engineer Emile de la Rey trained a neural network to recognize and isolate the voices of all four Beatles, training it on hundreds of hours of recordings, allowing him to extricate a specific voice from a recording.

That extrication, achieved with an assist from Paris Smaragdis of the University of Illinois, "re-synthed [the extricated vocal track] in a realistic way that matched trained samples of those instruments or voices in isolation," according to *Ars Technica*. "In other words, the AI recreates the target voice by merging the information from the tape with the model developed from already isolated samples of the same voice. It's not quite Lennon, but it's about as close as you can get."[3]

"We were able to take John's voice and get it pure through this AI, so that then we could mix the record as you would normally do," Paul said. "So, it gives you some sort of leeway."

"All of this is kind of scary," he concluded, "but exciting – because it's the future."

---

[3] The same technique was used to isolate Lennon's vocal on the classic Beatles recording "I've Got a Feeling", which Paul then used on his 2022 US tour, allowing him to do a virtual duet, live in concert, with his old partner.

"Glorified Tape Recorders"

Not everyone in the scientific world thinks the dangers of AI are the big news in the digital realm these days. Michio Kaku, theoretical physicist and frequent science commentator, told CNN recently that today's generative AI chatbots are nothing more than "glorified tape recorders", and that the public is overrating them a great deal.

"It takes snippets of what's on the web created by a human, splices them together and passes it off as if it created these things," he said. "And people are saying, 'Oh my God, it's a human, it's humanlike.'"

"This isn't intelligence," he'd told NBC earlier. "This is basically a sort of warped mirror of what's on the internet for the last 20 years...designed to spit out things that seem plausible."

His reactions stands far apart from those recorded elsewhere in this book, prognostications of doom and dread. Per Kaku, they are all misguided.

Humanity, he told CNN, is headed toward much more important change in the near future. We will be moving to a third stage of technological reality.

The first, he said, was our *analog stage* - "when we computed with sticks, stones, levers, gears, pulleys, string." Then came our current stage, the *digital*, which is about electricity, transistors, microprocessors.

Next up, the third stage: the *quantum realm*.

"Mother Nature would laugh at us because Mother Nature does not use zeros and ones," he said. "Mother Nature computes on electrons, electron waves, waves that create molecules. And that's why we're now entering stage three."

Quantum computing is the next step in computer technology, taking us beyond the mere digital. It will move the paradigm of computing beyond 0s and 1s, *bits*, into the realm of the *qubit*, which is based on the concept of quantum *superposition* – the simultaneous representations of more than one state.

Such a computer would operate on a scale many orders of magnitude beyond what even the fastest digital computers ever built could achieve. And that would lead to computers capable of miracles we currently only associate with AI; Kaku's point is that we're going to have computers so powerful that we won't even *need* AI.

We'll review the possibilities later on.

AI Meets Bach

Generative AI can produce not only human-like text responses and serviceable artwork, but music, as well. There are already plenty of AI apps out there that can crank out a royalty-free tune for you, on demand.

The tech underlying generative AI – the neural network – can also be trained to generate very specific music: for instance, music written in the style of Johann Sebastian Bach.

Gaetan Hadjeres and Francois Pachet, of the Sony Computer Science Laboratories in Paris, recently created a neural network called DeepBach to create Bach-like chorale compositions. Like all neural networks, DeepBach was trained on real-world data – in this case, more than 300 of the real Bach's chorales.

DeepBach can fool human experts about half the time, according to the *MIT Technology Review*. And it builds on earlier successes: Pachet's Flow Machine AI can actually analyze the style of a composer and then generate new, original works in that style. There's "Daddy's Car", for instance, an attempt to create a new song in the style of the Beatles.

And it can flip the process on its head, reimagining an existing work – Beethoven's "Ode to Joy", for example – in the style of the Beatles' "Penny Lane".

Not everyone is thrilled by this turn of events.

Douglas Hofstadter, one of AI's pioneers, was around for a similar breakthrough in the Nineties – EMI, the Experiments in Musical Intelligence program – and we read what he had to say about that in the first *Pod Bay Doors* volume:

"Ever since I was a child, music has thrilled me and moved me to the very core," he told a roomful of Google engineers. "And every piece that I love feels like it's a direct message from the emotional heart of the human being who composed it. It feels like it is giving me access to their innermost soul. And it feels like there is *nothing* more human in the world than the expression of music. Nothing. The idea that pattern manipulation of the most superficial sort can yield things that sound as if they are coming from a human being's heart is very, very troubling."☐

Well, as may be, music created by generative AI is as certain to be around from now on as its text and art peers. If even musicologists can be fooled by the quality of AI's Bach fakes, then AI-generated music is going to be more than adequate for the purposes of businesses that would rather pay next to nothing for the product, as opposed to paying a human composer to write it, on top of the cost of producing it.

For better or worse, this is how it's going to be now.

The AI compositions can be heard here:

https://www.openculture.com/2016/09/artificial-intelligence-program-tries-to-write-a-beatles-song-listen-to-daddys-car.html

https://www.openculture.com/2018/01/artificial-intelligence-writes-a-piece-in-the-style-of-bach.html

Google's News Machine

As the AP is taking ChatGPT on board, Google is working the news industry from the other side – creating product fine-tuned for journalism.

The tech behemoth has created a new AI tool called Genesis that consumes public information and turns it into news stories. The idea, according to Google's representatives, is that Genesis can be a "kind of personal assistant for journalists, automating some tasks to free time up for others."

Well, that's the goal of *most* workplace AI, so the intent can be faulted. But there has been some natural unease with the idea of AI generating content that might be labeled *news*. Don't we have enough trouble with untrustworthy content already?

We noted above that CNET has already been severely dinged for publishing inaccurate, AI-generated content; so has Gizmo and Buzzfeed. And not just for inaccuracy, but for plagiarism.

Journalists themselves are not happy.

"This could be incredibly dangerous for journalism as a business, especially if Google acts to juice its own search results to prioritize AI content," tweeted Gabe Rosenberg, a radio editor in Kansas City. "And worse yet is what these large media companies are already doing to screw over actual human workers."

"Let it be said, journalists don't need Google to write their articles as a 'personal assistant,'" tweeted Jessica Lessin of *The Information*. "Anything that Google (or any AI) could write has no real original reporting value."

Google insists that everyone is missing the point.

"Quite simply, these tools are not intended to, and cannot, replace the essential role journalists have in reporting, creating and fact-checking their articles," said Google's Jenn Crider to the *New York Times*. "For instance, AI-enabled tools could assist journalists with options for headlines or different writing styles."

Ironically, Google's own AI chatbot, Bard, has recently been outed as not being able to tell fact from fiction.

The hidden agenda, it's easy to suspect, is that the owners of media companies see AI as an opportunity to reduce head count (as owners in every industry seem to). The media company *Insider*, as it turns out, let 10 percent of its staff go in favor of generative AI.

It's not yet clear how this will all play out; but there's more at stake here than reducing a media company's annual outlay for salaries. As Futurism has pointed out in its reportage on this, it could ultimately be much more about reputation.

Norway, Getting It Right

The state of AI in the US is precarious; it looms dark over the economy, as the forecast of 300 million jobs vanishing in 10 years enters our national story. We are faced with a vast and terrible displacement that will wreak social havoc, and we are shackled to a political machine that will be all but useless in charting a course through the resulting morass.

But elsewhere, the picture isn't so grim. Some countries are already getting AI right. Out front on this one is Norway.

Situated in Northern Europe on the Scandinavian Peninsula with Sweden and Finland, Norway quietly leads the civilized world in many domains. It is breathtakingly beautiful, clean, and prosperous, falling in the Top 10 of the Highest Quality of Life Index and Highest Human Development Index (the US isn't on either list). It's No. 4 on the world-wide GDP-per-capita list (the US is No. 8). And it's where they hand out the Nobel Peace Prize every year.

Its five million inhabitants enjoy top-notch public infrastructure, including the fastest mobile Internet connectivity in the world. Not surprising in the country that built the longest tunnel on Earth.

Norway is clearly a place where they get things right. And, per Forbes, AI is one of those things.

In Norway, the government has negotiated a partnership between the country's industry and academia to form a collective AI research community committed to the safe, effective development and deployment of new technology. This alliance – NORA, the Norwegian Artificial Intelligence Research Consortium – is all-inclusive, covering AI, robotics, machine learning, and other related disciplines. There are 16 members, including the nation's leading universities and research labs.

The dysfunction and distrust that pervade the national political and social discourse in the US doesn't exist in Norway. Its citizens place high levels of well-earned faith and confidence in both its public institutions and private industry. And it's in this healthy context that the Norwegian government has committed to a set of guidelines to which NORA has committed:

- artificial intelligence that is developed and used in Norway should be built on ethical principles and respect human rights and democracy;
- research, development and use of artificial intelligence in Norway should promote responsible and trustworthy AI;
- development and use of AI in Norway should safeguard the integrity and privacy of the individual;
- cyber security should be built into the development, operation and administration of AI solutions; and
- supervisory authorities should oversee that AI systems in their areas of supervision are operated in accordance with the principles for responsible and trustworthy use of AI

Associated tech challenges that vex the US and seem to defy solution, such as data privacy, are already high priorities receiving serious attention there; data privacy in particular is overseen by the Norwegian Data Protection Authority, which has created and distributed guidelines for the handling of metadata and implementation of effective data stewardship, requiring that organizations of all kinds take responsibility for managing their data well in-house, with attention to the legal issues surrounding its governance.

Another big AI/data problem in the US is that of bias in datasets, which can corrupt even the most well-meaning AI development effort, leaving the resulting app untrustworthy and even possibly malicious. The NDPA provides guidance in avoiding that bias.

There is also the problem of 'black box' AI, the product of deep learning processes that produce inscrutable algorithms that lack transparency. While the NDPA has no canned solution for that problem, it has not been shy about communicating the seriousness of the problem, in turn encouraging NORA to address it.

All of this is not to inspire a wave of Norway Envy; it's simply a ray of hope to suggest that however dire the AI picture might be today, we have strong evidence that it is possible to get it right, if we'll just pay close attention to those who are doing it better.

Human vs. AI Art

My youngest daughter is a fine arts major, deeply immersed in her training to become an animator. She is incensed at the intrusion of AI into her domain, and hasn't been shy about letting me know that.

She isn't the only one, of course; the entire motion picture industry is grinding to a halt over, among other things, the prospect of AI coming in and writing scripts and even replacing live actors. AI is essentially intruding into a domain that we humans thought we had all to ourselves: *creativity*.

Lucas Bellaiche and his team at Duke University took up the question in a study recently published in *Cognitive Research: Principles and Implications*. "Humans versus AI: whether and why we prefer human-created compared to AI-created artwork" addresses that question directly, delivering an unsurprising answer: yes, we prefer human-generated art.

As a rule, most people view art as a distinctly human thing, given its role in our emotional expression and its place in our narratives. Both privately and collectively, we value art because we see within it our own reflection. There's a passive assumption embedded in those emotions that, well, art belongs to us.

And now AI is challenging that assumption with its ability to create perfectly serviceable art, for a wide range of purposes, at the touch of a button.

"The topic is interesting because it shows the massive developments of AI in recent years," Bellaiche told *PsyPost*, "but what I am personally most interested in is actually the opportunity to explore what "creativity" even means to the layperson: is it a form of cognition that can be achieved by anything (including AI), or is it reserved for humans only, as a sort of valued anthropocentrism? What factors of creativity (in this case, art specifically) can be achieved by AI as compared to humans?"

The study included 149 participants who rated artwork they were presented with in terms of liking, beauty, profundity, and worth. There were 30 pieces of this artwork, each tagged either "human-created" or "AI-created". In fact, *all* of the art was AI-created, so the pro-human bias was clearly being triggered by the tag. The bias held firm over all four of the study criteria.

Bellaiche listed two takeaways.

"Firstly, we reinforce that art serves two purposes: The first function is the very surface-level enjoyment of art afforded through the senses – the visual (or auditory, for music) properties can be pretty, ugly, symmetrical, etc, and we respond to that by simple 'liking' or judgements of 'beauty.' The second function is more complex: art serves as a communicative medium from artist to audience. What does the art tell us? Is there a deeper meaning besides what we simply see/hear? What emotion is being conveyed?

"Secondly, importantly, art presumed to be by AI seems to do well on this first function (judgements of simple "liking" and "beauty" are nearly equal to art presumed to be by humans; i.e., AI can indeed make a pretty picture), but not so much on the second function."

"That is, the average person does not believe AI, compared to humans, to be able to communicate deep meaning very well through art, like emotions, narratives, worth, or profundity. Arguably, for people that are anti-AI, this should come as a relief, in that communicative properties of art will seemingly be reserved for the human and human only, on average."

My daughter, then, can indulge in a feeling of relief: most people, it would seem, would rather see her work than that of a computer. For now, at least, AI-generated art is nothing more than a convenience, rendered to innocuous ends; the human product is what has value in the eye of the beholder.

Capitalists will not see it this way, of course, and it remains possible – even probable – that this might someday change.

But not today.

No AI Copyrights!

Later, we'll look at how the Writer's Guild of America is rebelling against the threat of movie studios to replace screenwriters with generative AI. Today, it looks like the US Copyright Office is standing with the writers.

In the summer of 2023, Stephen Thaler, CEO of Imagination Engines, brought a lawsuit in contest of a ruling that content he had created via generative AI was ineligible for copywrite protection. The lawsuit argued that Thaler should be acknowledged "as an author where it otherwise meets authorship criteria," and that the Copyright Office's denial was "arbitrary, capricious, an abuse of discretion and not in accordance with the law.

The question at hand: is artwork generated solely by a computer eligible for copyright protection?

US District Judge Beryl Howell said No.

In her opinion, copyright law is not intended to "protect works generated by new forms of technology operating absent any guiding human hand... Human authorship is a bedrock requirement."

Thaler's interest goes beyond this particular copyright application: he is taking point for his entire industry, which has a lot riding on this question. Imagination Engines builds neural networks, and its generative AI Creativity Machine created a piece of art called *A Recent Entrance to Paradise* – which he then attempted to copyright.

The Copyright Office's denial of the application stated that "the nexus between the human mind and creative expression" is central to the point of copyright protection.

Howell's opinion reinforced this position, stating that copyright law "protects only works of human creation." Creativity is "at the core of copyrightability, even as that human creativity is channeled through new tools or into new media."

She further wrote that copyrights are "forms of property that the government was established to protect, and it was understood that recognizing exclusive rights in that property would further the public good by incentivizing individuals to create and invent... [encouraging] human individuals to engage in [creating]."

"The act of human creation - and how to best encourage human individuals to engage in that creation, and thereby promote science and the useful arts - was thus central to American copyright from its very inception."

On the other hand, the copyright office has allowed that while AI-generated content is not eligible for copyright protect, AI-assisted content can potentially qualify for copyright if it is included in the content of works created by a human being, "selected and arranged [in a] sufficiently creative way that the resulting work constitutes an original work of authorship."

Echoes of Asimov, part II

In the previous volume, we included the fun experiment of asking ChatGPT to write a short screenplay in the spirit of Isaac Asimov's "The Bicentennial Man" - a story about a robot living in a suburban home with mom, dad, and the kids, and assimilating as one of the family. ChatGPT came through, serving up a script that was true to the request (if not particularly inspired).

So here follows another such experiment, nudging ChatGPT to create something more complex – a story that echoes the theme of Asimov's masterpiece, "Nightfall".

☐

"Write a short story about a scientist on a planet where the stars only come out once every 2,000 years, and civilization is destroyed with every nightfall, then to be rebuilt. The scientist suspects that the coming nightfall will cause it to happen again, and tries to warn his colleagues that they must prepare for the worst."

Dr. Gabriel Arden stood atop the highest peak of Astoria, his home planet, gazing up at the vast expanse of the evening sky. The sun was setting, casting a warm golden hue over the landscape. It was a sight that would fill anyone's heart with tranquility, but for Gabriel, it brought a heavy sense of unease.

Astoria was a peculiar planet, known for its extraordinary celestial phenomenon. Unlike other worlds, the stars only revealed themselves once every 2,000 years. But there was a terrible price to pay for this breathtaking spectacle. As night fell, civilization crumbled, reduced to ruins by forces unknown. And as the sun rose, the world was born anew, and mankind would rebuild their cities and lives from the ashes of their past.

Gabriel, a brilliant scientist, had spent countless years studying the peculiar cycle. He had meticulously analyzed historical records and observed the patterns of destruction. As the next nightfall approached, his heart filled with dread. The signs were there, the subtle tremors beneath the surface, the increased frequency of natural disasters, and the eerie stillness that lingered in the air.

Fearing the impending disaster, Gabriel gathered his colleagues, the brightest minds of Astoria, in the grand halls of the Observatory of Wisdom. They all looked at him expectantly, their faces a mix of curiosity and concern.

"My friends," Gabriel began, his voice steady but laced with urgency. "We stand on the brink of another nightfall, and I fear it will bring devastation once again. We must prepare, plan, and protect our civilization from the chaos that awaits."

The room fell into an uneasy silence. Some scientists exchanged skeptical glances, unsure if they could trust Gabriel's intuition. After all, the nightfall was a part of their history, a recurring calamity they had learned to accept as an inevitable cycle of life and death.

Dr. Isabella Hartley, Gabriel's longtime colleague and closest friend, stepped forward, her voice filled with concern. "Gabriel, I respect your intellect, but we have endured this cycle for millennia. Our ancestors rebuilt, and so will we. Is there any concrete evidence to support your claim?"

Gabriel's eyes gleamed with determination. "I've studied the ancient texts, analyzed the patterns, and scrutinized the geological data.

 There's a growing instability in the planet's core, unlike anything we've seen before. If we don't heed the warning signs, this nightfall will be worse than any we've experienced. We must take precautionary measures to protect our people."

The room erupted with whispers and murmurs. Some scientists appeared intrigued, while others remained skeptical. But Gabriel refused to give up. He knew time was running out, and he needed their support.

"Listen, my friends," Gabriel implored, his voice rising above the commotion. "We have the knowledge and the technology to mitigate the destruction. We must fortify our cities, create underground shelters, and devise a plan to rebuild swiftly. If we unite and prepare, we can emerge stronger from this catastrophe."

His words hung in the air, the weight of their decision pressing down on each scientist's shoulders. Slowly, one by one, they nodded, acknowledging the truth in Gabriel's words. They trusted his expertise and knew that their very survival depended on their willingness to act.

Together, they rallied the people of Astoria, spreading the urgent message of the impending nightfall. With unparalleled determination, they worked day and night, constructing shelters, reinforcing infrastructure, and developing emergency protocols. The once-skeptical scientists now stood united with Gabriel, their collective purpose guiding their every action.

As the final hours ticked away, the people of Astoria sought refuge in the safety of their fortified shelters. Gabriel, with a heavy heart, looked out over the city one last time, hoping that their preparations would be enough.

Then, as the sun dipped below the horizon, the stars began to emerge, casting an ethereal glow upon the land. The nightfall arrived, and with it came the wrath of destruction. Violent storms raged, earthquakes shook the foundations, and tsunamis swallowed coastlines.

But this time, the people of Astoria were ready. They huddled in their shelters, clinging to the hope Gabriel had instilled in them. And as dawn broke, revealing the battered landscape, they emerged, resolute and unyielding.

Gabriel stood among them, witnessing the devastation firsthand. His heart ached for the losses they had endured, but he also felt a glimmer of pride. Their preparations had paid off, and the city still stood, a testament to their resilience.

As the days passed, the people of Astoria worked tirelessly, rebuilding their homes, tending to their wounds, and reclaiming their lives.

Gabriel and his colleagues continued their scientific research, searching for answers that could further protect them in the future.

For on Astoria, a planet trapped in an endless cycle of destruction and rebirth, the stars would one day vanish again, and they would be ready, armed with knowledge, unity, and hope.

ChatGPT in the Chinese Room

One of the great thought experiments of the modern age cuts right to the heart of the AI discourse: can machines ever think like humans?

Many, of course, take for granted that they will. Because HAL-9000. And The Terminator. And Commander Data. But the belief burns even brighter among actual AI experts and practitioners; few are the technologists who *don't* think machines will one day become conscious.

"Whether we are based on carbon or silicon makes no fundamental difference," declares Dr. Chandra, HAL's creator, in *2010*.

This question had seized geek minds as far back as 1980, when Berkeley philosopher John Searle, invited to speak on the subject at an academic conference, constructed that great thought experiment while flying across the country.

The Chinese Room.

Imagine a closed room containing a human being and a set of reference books. On one end of this room is a slot through which a person outside the room can insert a slip of paper covered with Chinese characters. The person in the room doesn't understand Chinese; but they can nonetheless execute the task of looking up the characters in the books provided, follow the instructions in a rulebook that prescribes an appropriate series of Chinese characters constituting a response, and submit a slip of paper with those characters through the slot.

To the person on the outside, it would appear that the room understands Chinese. But the person inside the room doesn't.

This scenario, Searle argued, mimics the linear, symbol-driven computer programming of the time. The programs were static; the processor executing it was just a very fast calculator, likewise static. The *only* thing not static in the Chinese Room is the person - and they are restricted to a static, purely mechanical function.

If the person in the room doesn't understand Chinese, how could a microprocessor possibly do so?

In response to Searle's argument, the mob rose up in protest, and you could hardly hear yourself think for the roar of their bowels. Searle was declaring machine intelligence *fundamentally impossible*; and despite the complete absence of any proof to the contrary, this was considered a heresy.

Mind you, Searle wasn't saying anything of the sort; he was saying that digital processors and symbolic processing could never deliver machines that think like humans. In the 40 years since, of course, nothing to convince us otherwise has emerged.

His many critics were all over the map in their denunciations: sentience is 'emergent', they argued; but the Chinese Room is utterly static, while emergent systems are inherently dynamic (you can only have emergence in a system that changes). The person in the Chinese Room doesn't understand, but the *system* understands, they argued; no, the system can't connect the person's actual understanding, the product of their experience in the world, to whatever is going on the symbols to the 'system's' input and output. They're just symbols; from the room's standpoint, they have no meaning.

The debate has become a point of piety over the decades, with neither side budging an inch; it long ago devolved into a parlor game where Searle's opponents content themselves with inserting their own custom definitions of "understanding" into the argument, sidestepping its central point:

If the Chinese Room, as a system, doesn't have any understanding of the meaning of any of the symbols, then it is *purely syntactical*; *semantics* – meaning – are by definition absent. Searle's point is not that machines will never be able to think, or become conscious; it's that there can be no human-like thinking or consciousness without semantics, without meaning. A purely syntactical system can never think like a human, have intentionality, or become conscious, he still asserts today; if we had an AI that could even pass the Turing Test, interacting with us in English, it would still be empty inside, if it was purely syntactical. There would be no 'emergence'. It could never achieve consciousness.

And now... we have an AI that can pass the Turing Test. An AI that interacts with us in English (or any other language). An AI that even answers our questions.

ChatGPT, put simply, is the Chinese Room.

It does all the requisite symbol-mapping, and *it even does so without a rulebook* – the app is based on neural networks, not conventional programming of the sort Searle was discussing. *It can even learn* (though the learning is not part of the app itself, but the refresh process it undergoes during updates).

And no one who understands AI even a little bit, let alone those well-versed in deep learning and large language models, is about to argue that ChatGPT is sentient, or that it has any self-awareness or intentionality, or that any of these traits could possibly emerge – *even though it can learn*. On the contrary, these same people are loudly denouncing ChatGPT as nothing even close to sentient.

ChatGPT is semantically empty. It does not know the *meaning* of a single word submitted to it, nor a single word it offers in response.

For myself, I've supported Searle's argument all these decades, and been shouted down more times than I can count – by lettered academics, cock-sure IT professionals, and breathless, indignant fanboys. None of them have tried to defend ChatGPT as evidence that the Chinese Room is incorrect.

I'm not alone in holding up ChatGPT as evidence that it is. Just google "ChatGPT Chinese Room".

The Chinese Room has been, for more than 40 years, our standard metric for machine intelligence that truly rises to the level of our own. I submit that it has been replaced; ChatGPT far better illuminates the problem, and is stirring far more insights than its predecessor.

Really Bad Analogies Made by High School Students[4]

Her eyes were like two brown circles with big black dots in the center.

He was as tall as a 6'3" tree.

Her face was a perfect oval, like a circle that had its two sides gently compressed by a Thigh Master.

From the attic came an unearthly howl. The whole scene had an eerie, surreal quality, like when you're on vacation in another city and Jeopardy comes on at 7:00 p.m. instead of 7:30.

John and Mary had never met. They were like two hummingbirds who had also never met.

She had a deep, throaty, genuine laugh, like that sound a dog makes just before it throws up.

The ballerina rose gracefully en pointe and extended one slender leg behind her, like a dog at a fire hydrant.

---

[4] The relevance will soon become clear.

He was as lame as a duck. Not the metaphorical lame duck, either, but a real duck that was actually lame. Maybe from stepping on a land mine or something. Her vocabulary was as bad as, like, whatever.

She grew on him like she was a colony of E. coli and he was room-temperature Canadian beef.

The revelation that his marriage of 30 years had disintegrated because of his wife's infidelity came as a rude shock, like a surcharge at a formerly surcharge-free ATM.

The lamp just sat there, like an inanimate object.

McBride fell 12 stories, hitting the pavement like a Hefty bag filled with vegetable soup.

His thoughts tumbled in his head, making and breaking alliances like underpants in a dryer without Cling Free.

He spoke with the wisdom that can only come from experience, like a guy who went blind because he looked at asolar eclipse without one of those boxes with a pinhole in it and now goes around the country speaking at high schools about the dangers of looking at a solar eclipse without one of those boxes with a pinhole in it.

Long separated by cruel fate, the star-crossed lovers raced across the grassy field toward each other like two freight trains, one having left Cleveland at 6:36 p.m. traveling at

55 mph, the other from Topeka at 4:19 p.m. at a speed of 35 mph.

Shots rang out, as shots are wont to do.

The little boat gently drifted across the pond exactly the way a bowling ball wouldn't.

Her hair glistened in the rain like a nose hair after a sneeze.

The hailstones leaped from the pavement, just like maggots when you fry them in hot grease.

He fell for her like his heart was a mob informant and she was the East River.

She was as easy as the TV Guide crossword.

She walked into my office like a centipede with 98 missing legs.

The young fighter had a hungry look, the kind you get from not eating for a while.

He was deeply in love. When she spoke, he thought he heard bells, as if she were a garbage truck backing up.

Her date was pleasant enough, but she knew that if her life was a movie this guy would be buried in the credits as something like "Second Tall Man."

The thunder was ominous-sounding, much like the sound of a thin sheet of metal being shaken backstage during the storm scene in a play.

She caught your eye like one of those pointy hook latches that used to dangle from screen doors and would fly up whenever you banged the door open again.

Fishing is like waiting for something that does not happen very often.

The knife was as sharp as the tone used by Rep. Sheila Jackson Lee (D-Tex.) in her first several points of parliamentary procedure made to Rep. Henry Hyde (R-Ill.) in the House Judiciary Committee hearings on the impeachment of President William Jefferson Clinton.

Her eyes were shining like two marbles that someone dropped in mucus and then held up to catch the light.

I felt a nameless dread. Well, there probably is a long German name for it, like Geschpooklichkeit or something, but I don't speak German. Anyway, it's a dread that nobody knows the name for, like those little square plastic gizmos that close your bread bags. I don't know the name for those either.

She was as unhappy as when someone puts your cake out in the rain, and all the sweet green icing flows down and then you lose the recipe, and on top of that you can't sing worth a damn.

Her artistic sense was exquisitely refined, like someone who can tell butter from I Can't Believe It's Not Butter.

Bob was as perplexed as a hacker who means to access T:flw.quid55328.com\aaakk/ch@ung but gets T:\flw.quidaaakk/ch@ung by mistake.

You know how in "Rocky" he prepares for the fight by punching sides of raw beef? Well, yesterday it was as cold as that meat locker he was in.

The dandelion swayed in the gentle breeze like an oscillating electric fan set on medium.

Her lips were red and full, like tubes of blood drawn by an inattentive phlebotomist.

The sunset displayed rich, spectacular hues like a .jpeg file at 10 percent cyan, 10 percent magenta, 60 percent yellow and 10 percent black.

The Barrier of Meaning

One thing AI is today – today being 2023 – is *narrow*. Individual AIs are very good at doing *one thing well*. Very, very well, often much better than human beings. What AI today isn't is... general. We don't have general AI. AGI.

That's the state of AI today: we have narrow AI, and look to the future for general AI. We don't yet know for sure what it will look like. But we know what it must include.

ChatGPT has made clear what the Chinese Room has been saying for decades: AI that can do what human beings can do requires more than just symbols and rules; there needs to be *meaning*.

AI expert Melanie Mitchell – ironically, student of Douglas Hofstadter, who speaks out against the Chinese Room argument to this day, quotes mathematician/philosopher Gian-Carlo Rota: "I wonder whether or when AI will crash the barrier of meaning."

The *barrier of meaning*. Where AI is concerned – and AI that can truly think, truly equal the performance of the human mind, and ultimately achieve self-awareness – there is no greater barrier. AI must acquire *meaning* to achieve any of those goals.

And per Hofstadter and Mitchell, and their years of work together at Hofstadter's Center for Research on Concepts and Cognition, the essential ingredient in *meaning* is *analogy*.

The engine of human thought and understanding, in this formulation, is our ability to acquire knowledge in one domain and transfer it to another. We are able to see similarities between objects and events in the world around us, and in so doing, make connections that generate a large and *general* body of knowledge and understanding.

"It's understanding the essence of a situation by mapping it to another situation that is already understood," she told *Scientific American*. "If you tell me a story and I say, 'Oh, the same thing happened to me,' literally the same thing did not happen to me that happened to you, but I can make a mapping that makes it seem very analogous. It's something that we humans do all the time without even realizing we're doing it. We're swimming in this sea of analogies constantly."

That transfer of knowledge from one domain to another – and the internal world-building that results – are beyond the current reach of AI.

"Today's state-of-the-art neural networks are very good at certain tasks," she said, "but they're very bad at taking what they've learned in one kind of situation and transferring it to another"—the essence of analogy.

"It's a fundamental mechanism of thought that will help AI get to where we want it to be. Some people say that being able to predict the future is what's key for AI, or being able to have common sense, or the ability to retrieve memories that are useful in a current situation. But in each of these things, analogy is very central.

"For example, we want self-driving cars, but one of the problems is that if they face some situation that's just slightly distant from what they've been trained on they don't know what to do. How do we humans know what to do in situations we haven't encountered before? Well, we use analogies to previous experience. And that's something that we're going to need these AI systems in the real world to be able to do, too."

This approach, which Mitchell is deep-diving at the Sante Fe Institute and to which Hofstadter has devoted his entire career, is being under-studied in AI research, she said, because AI researchers "haven't recognized its essential importance to cognition.

"Focusing on logic and programming in the rules for behavior—that's the way early AI worked. More recently people have focused on learning from lots and lots of examples, and then assuming that you'll be able to do induction to things you haven't seen before using just the statistics of what you've already learned. They hoped the abilities to generalize and abstract would kind of come out of the statistics, but it hasn't worked as well as people had hoped.

"You can show a deep neural network millions of pictures of bridges, for example, and it can probably recognize a new picture of a bridge over a river or something. But it can never abstract the notion of 'bridge' to, say, our concept of 'bridging the gender gap'. These networks, it turns out, don't learn how to abstract. There's something missing. And people are only sort of grappling now with that."

She acknowledges that part of the problem is that we're not totally clear on the definition of what it is we're trying to create.

"This word 'understand' is one of these suitcase words that no one agrees what it really means," she said, "almost like a placeholder for mental phenomena that we can't explain yet. But I think this mechanism of abstraction and analogy is key to what we humans call understanding. It is a mechanism by which understanding occurs. We're able to take something we already know in some way and map it to something new."

This is like *that*...

Hofstadter's thesis: the engine of intelligence, in humans and other creatures, is the ability to see that *This* is like *That*.

Analogy.

The ability of the brain to look at an object, take in a scene, observe an event, hear a word, and immediately relate it to some other object, scene, event or word remembered from previous experience is, of course, *analogy* – realizing that *This* is like *That*. It is a simple, unobtrusive thought, so passive and inconsequential that it seems to barely merit mention beyond the domains of literature and public speaking. But Hofstadter has for decades maintained that analogy – *This* is like *That* – pervades every layer of our cognition and consciousness, providing the brain with all that matters.

Analogy, he has written, *is the core of cognition*.

His 2013 book *Surfaces and Essences* is subtitled *Analogy as the Fuel and Fire of Thinking*.

His 1995 book *Fluid Concepts and Creative Analogies* presented *Computer Models of the Fundamental Mechanisms of Thought*, concocted by himself and his students in the Fluid Analogies Research Group at Indiana University.

And *GEB* itself, published all the way back in 1979, posits analogy and metaphor as the underpinnings of *concepts* (certainly central to both cognition and consciousness) - an idea not completely original, but developed with great sophistication in Hofstadter's work.

"I've managed to convince myself that analogy is really at the core of thinking — not just for myself, but for other people, too," he told *Wired* magazine in 1995. "I'm trying to put forth a vision of thought that involves — if you don't want to say 'analogy-making' you can say 'stripping away irrelevancies to get at the gist of things.' I feel I've discovered something essential about what thinking is, and I'm on a crusade to make it clear to everybody."

Despite his loner status, Hofstadter has many allies in this domain:

"Our conceptual networks are intricately structured by analogical and metaphorical mappings, which play a key role in the synchronic construction of meaning and in its diachronic evolution," wrote Gilles Fouconnier in *Mappings in Thought and Language*. "Parts of such mappings are so entrenched in everyday thought and language that we do not consciously notice them; other parts strike us as novel and creative. The term *metaphor* is often applied to the latter, highlighting the literary and poetic aspects of the phenomenon. But the general cognitive principles at work are the same, and they play a key role in thought and language at all levels."

"Intelligence," wrote Jeff Hawkins in *On Intelligence*, "is the capacity of the brain to predict the future by analogy to the past."

"I think that metaphor really is a key to explaining thought and language," wrote Steven Pinker in *The Stuff of Thought*. "The human mind comes equipped with an ability to penetrate the cladding of sensory appearance and discern the abstract construction underneath — not always on demand, and not infallibly, but often enough and insightfully enough to shape the human condition. Our powers of analogy allow us to apply ancient neural structures to newfound subject matter, to discover hidden laws and systems in nature, and not least, to amplify the expressive power of language itself."

Even the revered Marvin Minsky weighs in:

"The ability to consider differences between differences is important because it lies at the heart of our abilities to solve new problems," he wrote in *The Society of Mind*. "This is because these 'second-order-differences' are what we use to remind ourselves of other problems we already know how to solve. Sometimes this is called 'reasoning by analogy' and is considered to be an exotic or unusual way to solve problems. But in my view, it's our most ordinary way of doing things."

"Every thought is to some degree a metaphor," he goes on to say, "Most of our ordinary mental work - that is, our commonsense reasoning - is based more on 'thinking by analogy' - that is, applying to our present circumstances our representations of seemingly similar previous experiences."

This and *That*

"One of my firmest conclusions is that we always think by seeking and drawing parallels to things we know from our past," Hofstadter wrote in *I Am a Strange Loop*, "and that we therefore communicate best when we exploit examples, analogies, and metaphors galore, when we avoid abstract generalities, when we use very down-to-earth, concrete, and simple language, and when we talk directly about our own experience."

Analogy is thus the moving part in intelligence – and, by extension, consciousness – that connects new information about the world to an individual's experience. When *This* is like *That*, our experiential knowledge of *That* is transferred to *This* – placing analogy at the epicenter of learning – and, by extension, understanding. Analogia.

"How do we ever understand anything?" asked Marvin Minsky. "Almost always, I think, by using one or another kind of analogy - that is, by representing each new thing as though it resembles something we already know. Whenever a new thing's internal workings are too strange or complicated to deal with directly, we represent whatever parts of it we can in terms of more familiar signs. This way, we make each novelty seem similar to some more ordinary thing. It really is a great discovery, the use of signals, symbols, words, and names. They let our minds transform the strange into the commonplace."

"Nothing unknown can ever become known except through its analogy with other things known," wrote Charles Peirce in *Logic, Considered as Semeiotic*, way back in 1902.

And finally, "...metaphor is not a mere extra trick of language, as it is so often slighted in the old schoolbooks on composition; it is the very constitutive ground of language," from Julian Jaynes in *The Origin of Consciousness in the Breakdown of the Bicameral Mind*. "I am using metaphor here in its most general sense: the use of a term for one thing to describe another because of some kind of similarity between them or between their relations to other things."

Hofstadter takes this basic assumption about the role of analogy and embeds it below the level of conscious thought; in his account, few if any human thoughts are completely analogy-free, and particularly not those written down: "In the final analysis," he wrote in the introduction to *Strange Loop*, "virtually every thought in this book (or in any book) is an analogy, as it involves recognizing something as being a variety of something else."

He goes on to single out analogy as the very engine of meaning: each new thing we experience is imbued with meaning by the known thing we map it to; and the new thing has the potential to add meaning to the old thing.

Manipulations

So powerful is the mechanism of analogy, Hofstadter insists, that it can control us; and we, in turn, can use it as a form of control.

Analogies control us in two ways: first, they often operate below the level of conscious thought. Recognition, perception, familiarity – each of these is a reflexive response or feeling, and they all have analogy at their core. The degree to which we achieve a sense of understanding of a new object or experience or encounter is inevitably constrained by the passive analogies that click into place beneath our attention. Second, our overt interpretations are similarly constrained, as analogy trims them down to a small subset of all that are possible. Moreover – and more insidiously! - they potentially preordain our conclusions, as they blind us to possibilities that might be beyond our experience or understanding.

"The fact is, the interpretation of a situation is inseparable from the analogies (or categories) it evokes," he wrote in *Surfaces and Essences*. "Our categories are thus organs of perception; they extend our physiological senses, allowing us to 'touch' the external world in a more abstract fashion."

And how do we use analogies for manipulation?

One way is the *caricature analogy* - "a very common sort of cognitive act consisting in the dreaming-up of a new situation that differs greatly from the original one, at least on the surface, but which, at a deeper level, is 'exactly the same thing,' and which has aspects that cannot help nudging the listener towards the conclusion desired by the speaker."

He provides many examples:

"A woman needs a man like a fish needs a bicycle."

A scientist seeking a job abroad wrote to a colleague: "I love my country, but doing science here is like playing soccer with a bowling ball."

"Fighting for peace is like fucking for virginity."

"Trying to throw a fastball by Henry Aaron is like trying to sneak a sunrise past a rooster."

"Imagining relativity before the equation $E = mc^2$ was discovered is like imaging Pisa before the Tower of Pisa had been built."

Investment guru Warren Buffett commented that the huge profit-making opportunities opened up by the global financial crisis made him feel "like a hungry mosquito at a nudist camp."

These and other examples underscore Hofstadter's point beautifully: we are all very familiar with such caricature analogies, and most of us use them at least on occasion. They perform exactly as advertised: two things not even distantly connected, in literal interpretation, nest together perfectly in the abstract – and our lightbulb goes off, we understand. And very often, when presented with such analogies as arguments, we find ourselves persuaded, the actual merits of the argument aside.

Frequently, he points out, caricature analogy is the tool of the educator, for such analogies can have formidable explanatory force: countless schoolchildren have come to understand atoms as analogous to the solar system, and vice versa, for instance. And the very best public speakers tell stories from their own experience to connect with their audience and thereby communicate compelling general truths. The point being, sometimes manipulation-by-analogy is a healthy exercise, when the conclusion being slipped into the listener's mind is a useful and correct one.

Decisions, decisions

Analogy inhabits the core of all major life decisions, Hofstadter argues; taking a new job, marrying someone, moving to a new city, buying a car – all of these choices are rooted in analogia. When considering the new job/spouse/city/car, we immediately pull old jobs/spouses/cities/cars out of our experiential memory and map them as best we can, tallying up similarities and differences in service of our decision.

When the decision to be made involves something new, beyond our experience – changing careers for the first time, for instance, or moving from the city to the country – we still instinctively analogize, mapping not to our own experience but to things others have told us about their own similar experience. We can't *not* think that way, even if we end up deciding on some separate criteria.

"The idea is simple," Hofstadter wrote. "The only way we have of making decisions, whether they are small or large, is through analogy – that is, by making analogies with a spectrum of previous experiences (whether personal or vicarious) that have been brought to mind by the pressing decision."

If there is any remaining doubt that analogy lies at the heart of learning, intelligence, consciousness, a simple thought experiment may dispel it: imagine, just briefly, what life would be like without the power of analogy? What would happen to an individual's cognition if the ability to form analogies were suddenly removed?

Our perceptions would be crippled; no new experience would share meaning with any old experience.

Our communication would be decimated; we would lose the ability to convey our thoughts and experiences to others, or to make sense of theirs.

Our ability to learn would be obliterated; our minds would be repositories of random facts about the world, none of them related to any other.

In short, if there is no analogy, there is no intelligence, let alone consciousness.

"They are our means of applying the richness of our past experience to the present," he wrote. "Without them, we would flail about helplessly in the world."

This and *That* and *The Other* – and back to *This*

Analogia is not Hofstadter's only contribution to the understanding of consciousness; remember that he is a *strange loop* (he told us so in the title of his 2007 book), and as it happens, the latter depends inexorably on the former.

More precisely, Hofstadter – and by analogy, all human beings – are not just strange loops, but complex amalgams of strange loops. As defined above, a strange loop is a recursive cross-level feedback loop that navigates through a hierarchy of some kind – and such loops emerge within human thought, to the point of being passed from one person to another. That definition, by definition[2], hinges on the sharing of experience between individuals – and that means that strange loops are, necessarily, analogical:

This analogizes to *That*; *That* analogizes to *The Other*; then, out of the blue, *The Other* analogizes to *This*, or

This -> *That* -> *The Other* -> *This*...

...and, Hey Presto! We have a strange loop! Most strange loops emerge from just such a process.

But analogy is not always the bond between disparate things; sometimes analogy is variation on a theme:

This-A -> *This-B* -> *This-C* -> *This-D* and back to *This-A* ->, which covers vast territory, from the earworming of songs in a particular style to classical composition itself.

And that takes us deep into the potential of the strange loop, to wit:

This-A1 -> *This-B1* -> *This-C1* -> *This-D1* -> *This-A2* -> *This-B2* -> *This-C2* -> *This-D2* ...

...to the core of creativity itself. Strange loops formed in analogical steps can (and often do) depart from the actual, from experience, and exist completely within the imagination, giving rise to the creative process.

How, without analogia and strange loops, would creativity be possible? Creativity is the generation of something new from something old – analogy sits at the very center of the process, as one note or word or brushstroke inspires the next, one idea births another, one old solution is modified to solve a new problem. All of these are analogical events; and all become, necessarily, strange loops, as there is no separating the created thing from the perceptions and experiences that inspired it – even if those perceptions or experiences were not consciously surfaced in the creative act.

"And that is also the way the human mind works," wrote Hofstadter in *Strange Loop*, "by the compounding of old ideas into new structures that become new ideas that can themselves be used in compounds, and round and round endlessly, growing ever more remote from the basic earthbound imagery that is each language's soil."

Standard components

Without *This* is like *That*, without strange loops, intelligence and consciousness could not exist. Learning and understanding, if possible, would be static and ineffective in our dynamic and ever-changing physical landscape.

We can say, then, that analogia and strange loops qualify as *inherent* properties of intelligence and consciousness. And if they are required in a biological mind, they likewise would be required in a machine mind; for the claims of the previous paragraph would still prevail.

An experiential strange loop engine, whether brain or box, becomes conscious, given enough energy, capacity, and experience. It becomes an *I*.

"When and only when such a loop arises in a brain or in any other substrate, is a person-a unique new 'I' - brought into being," Hofstadter wrote in *GEB*. "Moreover, the more self-referentially rich such a loop is, the more conscious is the self to which it gives rise. Yes, shocking though this might sound, consciousness is not an on/off phenomenon, but admits of degrees, grades, shades. Or, to put it more bluntly, there are bigger souls and smaller souls.

"This is a liberating shift, because it allows one to move to a different level of considering what brains are: as media that support complex patterns that mirror, albeit far from perfectly, the world, of which, needless to say, those brains are themselves denizens - and it is in the inevitable self-mirroring that arises, however impartial or imperfect it may be, that the strange loops of consciousness start to swirl."

Convinced? Whatever your answer, don't stop thinking about this; even if analogy doesn't seem like the center of the target that Hofstadter and Mitchell (and I) believe it to be, it is still certainly very important in the AI story moving forward.

For one thing, being able to transfer knowledge from one domain to another without resorting to oceans of big data in the model-building process is going to streamline future development incredibly, reducing the cost of developing and training general AIs by orders of magnitude over today's methods.

For another, it will mean having AIs that can *truly* learn from themselves, drawing conclusions from their observations of new things without having to build them out explicitly. It will really be general intelligence.

Okay... where do we start?

That's a question that takes us out of the state of AI today and into AI's future – so we'll get to that later.

"I think we're not ready, I think we don't know what we're doing, and I think we're all going to die."

AI theorist Eliezer Yudkowsky

The Danger of AI

Much is made in the current hyped-up media about all the different ways AI can destroy human civilization: by making itself our overlord, or destroying our economy, or simply killing us all.

But the real threats are far subtler, and harder to recognize. Harder still to counter. Here are a few of the possibilities.

"We're All Going to Die!"

There's considerable entertainment value in Skynet Fever, the intense fears consuming and oozing from AI doomers everywhere as ChatGPT snarls like Cthulhu in the shadows of our browsers.

Now, there's plenty to be concerned as AI proliferates, and this section of the book serves up a lot of it. The trick is to figure out what's really a threat and how serious that threat might be.

"I think we're not ready, I think we don't know what we're doing, and I think we're all going to die," AI theorist Eliezer Yudkowsky told a pair of hosts on the *Bloomberg* web series *AI IRL* in the summer of 2023.

At face value, Yudkowsky is entertainment: he has actually called for the bombing of machine learning labs, so he may not be taken at first to be the voice of reason in this domain. But he's no spring chicken here; he's been studying the problem for decades, and formed his views with a great deal of study.

In the here-and-now, he is sounding the alarm over the fact that GPT-4, the LLM underlying ChatGPT, has inner workings that its own creators don't understand. This is, of course, an accepted feature of deep learning – *no* generative AI's inner workings are scrutable – but Yudkowsky sees this not as an inconvenience, but as cause for alarm.

"The state of affairs is that we approximately have no idea what's going on in GPT-4," he said. "We have theories but no ability to actually look at the enormous matrices of fractional numbers being multiplied and added in there, and [what those] numbers mean."

But this hasn't distracted him from his larger message, and when he talks about bombing machine learning labs, he's absolutely serious. You can read about it in a *Time* magazine article he wrote on the subject:

"The key issue is not "human-competitive" intelligence," he wrote, "it's what happens after AI gets to smarter-than-human intelligence. Key thresholds there may not be obvious, we definitely can't calculate in advance what happens when, and it currently seems imaginable that a research lab would cross critical lines without noticing.

"Many researchers steeped in these issues, including myself, expect that the most likely result of building a superhumanly smart AI, under anything remotely like the current circumstances, is that literally everyone on Earth will die. Not as in 'maybe possibly some remote chance,' but as in 'that is the obvious thing that would happen.' It's not that you can't, in principle, survive creating something much smarter than you; it's that it would require precision and preparation and new scientific insights, and probably not having AI systems composed of giant inscrutable arrays of fractional numbers.

Without that precision and preparation, the most likely outcome is AI that does not do what we want, and does not care for us nor for sentient life in general. That kind of caring is something that *could in principle* be imbued into an AI but *we are not ready* and *do not currently know how*."

If we end up with such AI, he wrote, we would stand no chance against it:

"The likely result of humanity facing down an opposed superhuman intelligence is a total loss," he wrote. "Valid metaphors include 'a 10-year-old trying to play chess against Stockfish 15', 'the 11th century trying to fight the 21st century,' and '*Australopithecus* trying to fight *Homo sapiens*'.

"To visualize a hostile superhuman AI, don't imagine a lifeless book-smart thinker dwelling inside the internet and sending ill-intentioned emails," he continued. "Visualize an entire alien civilization, thinking at millions of times human speeds, initially confined to computers - in a world of creatures that are, from its perspective, very stupid and very slow. A sufficiently intelligent AI won't stay confined to computers for long. In today's world you can email DNA strings to laboratories that will produce proteins on demand, allowing an AI initially confined to the internet to build artificial life forms or bootstrap straight to postbiological molecular manufacturing."

And that's how this King of the AI Doomers gets to his bomb-the-data-center conclusion. It makes more sense when spelled out that specifically. Here's his more-detailed plan for shutting AI down:

"The moratorium on new large training runs needs to be indefinite and worldwide," he wrote. "There can be no exceptions, including for governments or militaries. If the policy starts with the U.S., then China needs to see that the U.S. is not seeking an advantage but rather trying to prevent a horrifically dangerous technology which can have no true owner and which will kill everyone in the U.S. and in China and on Earth. If I had infinite freedom to write laws, I might carve out a single exception for AIs being trained solely to solve problems in biology and biotechnology, not trained on text from the internet, and not to the level where they start talking or planning; but if that was remotely complicating the issue I would immediately jettison that proposal and say to just shut it all down.

"Shut down all the large GPU clusters (the large computer farms where the most powerful AIs are refined). Shut down all the large training runs. Put a ceiling on how much computing power anyone is allowed to use in training an AI system, and move it downward over the coming years to compensate for more efficient training algorithms. No exceptions for governments and militaries. Make immediate multinational agreements to prevent the prohibited activities from moving elsewhere. Track all GPUs sold. If intelligence says that a country outside the agreement is building a GPU cluster, be less scared of a shooting conflict between nations than of the moratorium being violated; be willing to destroy a rogue datacenter by airstrike.

"Shut it all down," he concluded. "We are not ready. We are not on track to be significantly readier in the foreseeable future. If we go ahead on this everyone will die, including children who did not choose this and did not do anything wrong."

Yudkowsky's Bloomberg interview can be viewed here:

https://www.youtube.com/watch?v=VQNcZyQC6sM

His *Time* article may be read here:

https://time.com/6266923/ai-eliezer-yudkowsky-open-letter-not-enough/

"I think AI presents challenges to the traditional view of human consciousness. There are aspects of AI that develop by its own inner momentum and then have to be absorbed by human consciousness.

"Up to now philosophers and religious leaders would put forward concepts that science would then implement. With artificial intelligence, it could be the other way around."

~Dr. Henry Kissinger

Henry Kissinger and AI

When we think of prominent contemporary thinkers giving us their two cents about the advent of true AI, the name Henry Kissinger probably doesn't spring readily to mind.

But the ex-Secretary of State, multigenerational statesman and author of over a dozen books on geopolitics is, in fact, emerging as an AI thought leader, evidenced by his 2021 book *The Age of AI and our Human Future* (co-written by Eric Schmidt and Daniel Huttenlocher). He's been active in the AI domain for several years, driven in part by his interest in how AI affects the world political landscape; but as he has learned more about it, he sees AI as something more than just the latest technological chew toy for great nations to fight over.

"In the previous arms race, you could develop plausible theories about how you might prevail," he told Ted Koppel in an interview. "It's a totally new problem now."

That problem, in Kissinger's mind, extends beyond the fact of a new and transformative technology to the foundations of human cognition, which he believes will reshape human understanding and perception.

"Kissinger and his co-authors propose that AI's capacity to access realms of reality beyond human comprehension carries significant implications for our traditional notions of reason, knowledge, and choice," wrote Mohammed Soliman in a review of the book for *The National Interest*. "They contend that the technology's subtle influence on these foundational aspects of human cognition challenges the established worldview of the Enlightenment era and necessitates a reevaluation of our philosophical and ethical frameworks.

"'The essential difference between the Age of Enlightenment and the Age of AI is... not technological but cognitive,' Soliman quotes the book. "'After the Enlightenment, philosophy accompanied science. Bewildering new data and often counterintuitive conclusions, doubts, and insecurities were allayed by comprehensive explanations of the human experience. Generative AI is similarly poised to generate a new form of human consciousness."

In Kissinger, then, we have a whole new narrative – not Skynet Fever, not Utopia Waiting, but something else entirely: AI isn't just going to change our economics and politics, in his formulation; it will change our nature.

AI Rising

To begin, Kissinger is concerned with speed – both that of AI's rapid deployment in the real world, and how fast it can 'think', compared to human beings. Both of these rates are rapidly expanding.

"The speed with which artificial intelligence acts will make [human control] problematical in crisis situations," he told Koppel. In a military situation, for instance, "In relying on [AI's military decisions], we cannot double-check it, because we cannot review all the knowledge that the machine has acquired," he went on. "We are giving it that knowledge. But this will be one of the big debates. I am now trying to do what I did with respect to nuclear weapons, to call attention to the importance of the impact of this evolution."

AI will soon be out-thinking us, he warned. And that will affect our own thinking.

"I think AI presents challenges to the traditional view of human consciousness," he told *The Catalyst*. "There are aspects of AI that develop by its own inner momentum and then have to be absorbed by human consciousness. Last year I wrote an article in which I pointed out that up to now philosophers and religious leaders would put forward concepts that science would then implement. With artificial intelligence it could be the other way around. It presents realities at least in some of its manifestations."

Kissinger's three concerns

In a 2018 essay in *The Atlantic*, "How the Enlightenment Ends", Kissinger identified three major areas of concern about AI.

Unintended results

Because we don't fully understand what's going on inside an AI, we can never be fully certain we understand what it's doing (or why) - and we can't be fully certain that it understands what we want it to do.

"The danger [is] that AI will misinterpret human instructions due to its inherent lack of context."

Impact on human thought and values

Kissinger makes the point in the essay (and again in his book) that the gaming AIs AlphaGo and AlphaZero easily surpassed human performance by learning to play *without human guidance* (see above). They came up with game strategies that a human being might never even consider, once divorced from the perspective of human experts.

"AlphaGo defeated the world Go champions by making strategically unprecedented moves—moves that humans had not conceived and have not yet successfully learned to overcome. Are these moves beyond the capacity of the human brain? Or could humans learn them now that they have been demonstrated by a new master?"

AI surpassing our best and then becoming the teacher, rather than the student, means it will begin guiding our thinking, Kissinger fears.

AI will be inscrutable

Even when it is performing as expected and doing exactly as we asked, AI's lack of internal transparency will be a threat, Kissinger wrote.

"If its computational power continues to compound rapidly, AI may soon be able to optimize situations in ways that are at least marginally different, and probably significantly different, from how humans would optimize them," he believes. "But at that point, will AI be able to explain, in a way that humans can understand, why its actions are optimal? Or will AI's decision making surpass the explanatory powers of human language and reason? Through all human history, civilizations have created ways to explain the world around them - in the Middle Ages, religion; in the Enlightenment, reason; in the 19th century, history; in the 20th century, ideology. The most difficult yet important question about the world into which we are headed is this: What will become of human consciousness if its own explanatory power is surpassed by AI, and societies are no longer able to interpret the world they inhabit in terms that are meaningful to them?"

The end of the Enlightenment?

"If AI learns exponentially faster than humans, we must expect it to accelerate, also exponentially, the trial-and-error process by which human decisions are generally made: to make mistakes faster and of greater magnitude than humans do," he wrote. "It may be impossible to temper those mistakes, as researchers in AI often suggest, by including in a program caveats requiring "ethical" or "reasonable" outcomes. Entire academic disciplines have arisen out of humanity's inability to agree upon how to define these terms. Should AI therefore become their arbiter?

"The Enlightenment started with essentially philosophical insights spread by a new technology. Our period is moving in the opposite direction. It has generated a potentially dominating technology in search of a guiding philosophy. Other countries have made AI a major national project. The United States has not yet, as a nation, systematically explored its full scope, studied its implications, or begun the process of ultimate learning. This should be given a high national priority, above all, from the point of view of relating AI to humanistic traditions."

And that's a great concern, not just to Kissinger, but to many AI thinkers: are we investing enough attention and effort in the ethics of AI? Is the US falling behind the rest of the world in taking the risks of AI seriously, as Big Tech rockets forward with it?

"AI developers, as inexperienced in politics and philosophy as I am in technology, should ask themselves some of the questions I have raised here in order to build answers into their engineering efforts," he continued. "The US government should consider a presidential commission of eminent thinkers to help develop a national vision. This much is certain: If we do not start this effort soon, before long we shall discover that we started too late."

That presidential commission is soon to come, we think (see below), but it needs to be followed up with regulation and alliances, both domestic and international, to keep everyone on the same page.

A revolution in human affairs

AI "augurs a revolution in human affairs," Kissinger states in the book. A 2021 *Time* interview said, "The book argues that artificial intelligence processes have become so powerful, so seamlessly enmeshed in human affairs, and so unpredictable, that without some forethought and management, the kind of 'epoch-making transformations' they will deliver may send human history in a dangerous direction."

"What fascinates me is that we are moving into a new period of human consciousness which we don't yet fully understand," Kissinger told *Time*. "When we say a new period of human consciousness, we mean that the perception of the world will be different, at least as different as between the age of enlightenment and the medieval period, when the Western world moved from a religious perception of the world to a perception of the world on the basis of reason, slowly. This will be faster."

And he again used the Enlightenment as a referent:

"In the Enlightenment, there was a conceptual world based on faith," he said. "And so Galileo and the late pioneers of the Enlightenment had a prevailing philosophy against which they had to test their thinking. You can trace the evolution of that thinking.

"We live in a world which, in effect, has no philosophy; there is no dominant philosophical view. So the technologists can run wild. They can develop world-changing things, but there's nobody there to say, 'We've got to integrate this into something.'" - *something* being a societal framework, a cultural context, a way of thinking about that new thing that gives it a meaning and a value that allows us to inculcate it into human existence in a healthy way.

That missing something - a pure abstraction but a very real issue within the greater frame of how society evolves - might be the thing that disturbs Kissinger most: *Silicon Valley is now reshaping human consciousness.*

"I think the technology companies have led the way into a new period of human consciousness, like the Enlightenment generations did when they moved from religion to reason, and the technologists are showing us how to relate reason to artificial intelligence," he told *Time*. "It's a different kind of knowledge in some respects, because with reason - the world in which I grew up - each evidence supports the other. With artificial intelligence, the astounding thing is, you come up with a conclusion which is correct. But you don't know why. That's a totally new challenge. And so in some ways, what they have invented is dangerous. But it advances our culture. Would we be better off if it had never been invented? I don't know that. But now that it exists, we have to understand it. And it cannot be eliminated. Too much of our life is already consumed by it.

"I don't think we have examined this thoughtfully yet. If you imagine a war between China and the United States, you have artificial-intelligence weapons. Like every artificial intelligence, they are more effective at what you plan. But they might be also effective in what they think their objective is. And so if you say, 'Target A is what I want,' they might decide that something else meets these criteria even better. So you're in a world of slight uncertainty. Secondly, since nobody has really tested these things on a broad-scale operation, you can't tell exactly what will happen when AI fighter planes on both sides interact. So you are then in a world of potentially total destructiveness and substantial uncertainty as to what you're doing.

"World War I was almost like that in the sense that everybody had planned very complicated scenarios of mobilization, and they were so finely geared that once this thing got going, they couldn't stop it, because they would put themselves at a bad disadvantage."

We aren't ready

"The Deep Think computer was taught to play chess by playing against itself for four hours," Kissinger told *Time*. "And it played a game of chess no human being had ever seen before. Our best computers only beat it occasionally. If this happens in other fields, as it must and it is, that is something, and our world is not at all prepared for it.

"I don't know whether anyone could have foreseen how politics are changing as a result of it," he continued. "It may be the nature of the human destiny and human tragedy that they have been given the gift to invent things. But the punishment may be that they have to find the solutions themselves."

Hacking Civilization

Henry Kissinger's take on the true danger of AI – that it will alter human thinking and values – is shared by another influential contemporary thinker.

Yuval Noah Harari spends a great deal of time thinking about the future, and he's written quite a bit about it as well: his books *Sapiens: A Brief History of Mankind* and *Homo Deus: A Brief History of Tomorrow* are both hugely popular, and articulate very precise, nuanced views of where we're heading.

He's not at all certain that AI will help us more than hurt us.

In an article published in *The Economist*, Harari states that AI has "hacked the operating system" of human civilization. He's referring to generative AI's new human-like facility with text communication.

"Language is the stuff almost all human culture is made of. Human rights, for example, aren't inscribed in our DNA," he wrote. "Rather, they are cultural artifacts we created by telling stories and writing laws. Gods aren't physical realities. Rather, they are cultural artifacts we created by inventing myths and writing scriptures."

Our stories, our penchant for narrative and our ability to share information and worldview through language are what Harari means by the "operating system" of civilization. Having a new entity in the universe that can use it changes everything, he wrote.

Language is the foundation of human intimacy, he continued.

"Through its mastery of language, AI could even form intimate relationships with people and use the power of intimacy to change our opinions and worldviews," he wrote. We reviewed that idea above; it raises the question of just how seduced we can be by AI, and under what circumstances. Harari made his point by citing what happened to Blake Lemoine, the Google engineer who became convinced that the AI chatbot LaMDA had become sentient, and ended up losing his career. That's what AI can do already, Harari pointed out; what is yet to come?

The capacity of generative AI in leveraging emotion extends that danger into politics, where it could become the most potent tool yet for weaponizing harmful rhetoric in order to get people to vote a certain way. Similarly, it will be easily deployed to influence people emotionally to buy particular products. And he came alongside Bill Gates in predicting that generative AI could be used by bad actors to aggravate social and economic inequality.

Harari's essay calls for action, and job #1 for him is regulation that requires every AI to identify itself as an AI (a step that many others have called for; see above). He argues that AI tech, like nuclear technology before it, requires unified and coordinated international effort.

He goes so far as to say that our current social and political systems aren't capable of dealing with the challenge and potential threat of AI; therefore, we must change our social and political systems.

Is he right?

The Perfect Psychopath

We have long thought of AI as a someday source of support and guidance – that we would create for ourselves digital partners who would help us move forward into the future, consolidating our knowledge and bolstering our wisdom. (Google's "life coach" AI, discussed above, aspires to be such a partner.)

Increasingly, however, we see that we're not just going to be putting AI in an advisory role; we're going to be turning over a lot of our decision-making power to it.

How should we feel about that?

Guillaume Thierry, Professor of Cognitive Neuroscience at Bangor University, thinks we would be making a big mistake.

"One of the key reasons we shouldn't let AI have executive power is that it entirely lacks emotion, which is crucial for decision-making. Without emotion, empathy and a moral compass, you have created the perfect psychopath," he wrote on *The Conversation*. "The resulting system may be highly intelligent, but it will lack the human emotional core that enables it to measure the potentially devastating emotional consequences of an otherwise rational decision.

"There is essentially no limit," he continued, "to the number of positions of control from which it could exert unimaginable damage."

He acknowledges that AI has already penetrated every domain where the processing and analysis of information are crucial – which is to say, everything – and "this is where problems start – when we let AI systems take the critical step up from the role of adviser to that of executive manager."

For instance, "Instead of just suggesting remedies to a company's accounts, what if an AI was given direct control, with the ability to implement procedures for recovering debts, make bank transfers, and maximise profits – with no limits on how to do this. Or imagine an AI system not only providing a diagnosis based on X-rays, but being given the power to directly prescribe treatments or medication."

Thierry's concern is that no matter how proficient an AI might be at process management, when it comes to decision-making, it would lack a key component that we humans take for granted in our own decision-making: emotional intelligence.

Emotional intelligence helps us prioritize, weighing alternatives and their human consequences effectively; it helps us empathize with those impacted by our decisions, thereby influencing them; it helps us communicate. Any AI given control of big decisions with human consequences would need this quality; and, for now, AI utterly lacks it.

The popular example of an empathy-free AI implementing an effective decision with disastrous results is that of putting it in charge of fixing climate change: the AI would rightly conclude that human activity is the cause, and fix the problem by drastically reducing the human population.

Thierry's point is a good one, and should be taken under serious consideration. It will become easier and easier, moving forward, to turn decision-making power and control over to AI, as it becomes better than we are at process management. It will be cheaper than human control, too, making it inevitable.

But surely we can stay in the loop? Surely, acknowledging that even the most effective AI lacks our emotional intelligence, we can take steps to truly partner with it, and ensure that whatever it decides, we're right alongside?

Guardrails

The White House has its Blueprint for an AI Bill of Rights, and that's a powerful and useful step. But the job of regulating AI goes beyond just the White House.

Berkeley Professor Stuart Russell of the University of California famously framed the problem as follows:

"It's as if an alien civilization warned us by email of its impending arrival, and we replied, 'Humanity is currently out of the office'. Fortunately, humanity is now back in the office and has read the email."

"We don't have a lot of time," CEO Dario Amodei of San Francisco AI firm Anthropic told a US Senate committee. "Whatever we do, we have to do it fast."

All true. The problem: AI is advancing at an exponential pace – and US lawmakers move almost glacially.

But talks have begun. The Congressional response accompanying the White House's AI Bill of Rights has been hearings to get themselves educated, hearing testimony from many industry AI experts.

"We must approach AI with the urgency and humility it deserves," said Senate Majority Leader Chuck Schumer as he presented his SAFE Innovation Framework for AI.

In a rare moment of lucidity, House Majority Leader Kevin McCarthy likewise stepped up, requiring all members of the House Intelligence Committee to take AI courses.

"What you see here is not all that common, which is bipartisan unanimity," said Committee Chair Richard Blumenthal, who oversaw some of the hearings.

"There has to be a cop on the beat," he said. "That cop on the beat, in the AI context, has to be not only enforcing rules but also, as I said at the very beginning, incentivizing innovation – and sometimes funding it – to provide the air bags and seat belts and the crash-proof kinds of safety measures that we have in the automobile industry."

This sobriety and atypical bipartisan cooperation is a badly-needed response to an urgent situation, and has produced a number of positive initiatives:

- the creation of a regulatory agency to oversee the growth of AI and serve as guarantor of human interests over corporate profits
- the establishment of liability to hold AI developers responsible for their creations
- the requirement of transparency in AI models, such that they and their product are identified as AI (more on this later)

More than 20 AI-related bills have already made their way to the Senate and the House, covering government risk assessment of AI, the development of preparedness strategies, and other important topics. Many more will surely be following.

And sooner is better, when it comes to regulatory action: Stuart Russell and 250 of his peers recently signed the Statement on AI Risk, which stresses that the risk of human extinction from AI should be rated as high as the risk presented by pandemics and nuclear war.

You can read Schumer's SAFE Framework and the AI Risk statement here:

https://www.democrats.senate.gov/imo/media/doc/schumer_ai_framework.pdf

https://www.safe.ai/statement-on-ai-risk#open-letter

A More Convincing Liar

AI is already better at many things than human beings will ever be. Unfortunately, it seems to already be getting better at one thing we do that we shouldn't: lying.

We've endured profound social damage in the Internet age from the spread of disinformation that social media has so capably enabled. Now we have AI that can generate content of exactly the kind we routinely consume online, day to day. When AI is generating the content, and it includes disinformation, will we be able to spot it?

Not likely, according to a study by researchers at the University of Zurich. AI-generated disinformation is already more convincing than human-generated disinformation.

The study states that participants were 3% less likely to spot false tweets that have been written by AI than tweets composed by actual people.

Of course, 3% doesn't seem like much; but even if AI never gets better than dead-even, it's a monumental concern; and it's inconceivable that AI won't rapidly get much, much better.

"The fact that AI-generated disinformation is not only cheaper and faster, but also more effective, gives me nightmares," said Giovanni Spitale, who was in charge of the study. "He believes that if the team repeated the study with the latest large language model from OpenAI, GPT-4, the difference would be even bigger, given how much more powerful GPT-4 is."

The study included 697 people who were given an online quiz, rating tweets on their credibility. The tweets included 10 true tweets and 10 false ones that had been generated by GPT-3. These were presented along with human-generated tweets.

What's the explanation? Why does AI-generated disinformation seem more credible than the human kind?

"GPT-3's text tends to be a bit more structured when compared to organic [human-written] text," Spitale said. "But it's also condensed, so it's easier to process."

Whatever the reason, it's a distressing thought: it's already *cheaper* for bad actors to generate content that can be used to mislead and manipulate those who consume it; if that content is also *more effective*, that makes it all the more certain we're going to be dealing with a great deal of it.

Executive Orders

The Biden Administration's Blueprint for an AI Bill of Rights, mentioned above, has progressive activists calling for action.

As we saw, that document is non-binding; it's basically just a wish list, and until it's anything more than that, AI will roll onward, growing exponentially, without any regulation.

The Center for American Progress thinks that isn't good enough, and has called for the president to do the following:

- Create a White House Council on Artificial Intelligence;
- Ensure that all AI tools used by federal agencies or their contractors be evaluated under the AI Risk Management Framework articulated by the National Institute of Standards and Technology;
- Put together a plan to deal with AI economic impact (the loss of millions of jobs, in particular);
- Require that the White House Competition Council enforce fair competition in the AI market.

☐
Those are all very, very good ideas. But they will have to be authoritatively put in motion, and we can't expect a congress lost in the early 20th century to approve such measures. They will require executive orders.

"The brisk pace of AI development does not mean that there is nothing that can be done to steer emerging technologies onto a path that benefits society," said Alondra Nelson, the former acting director of the White House Office of Science and Technology Policy, who oversaw the writing of the Blueprint. She is now a distinguished senior fellow at CAP.

Adam Conner, CAP's vice president for technology policy, supports her push for executive orders:

"One of the real powers of a new AI executive order is the U.S. government can choose how to implement and live its values in its own usage of AI."

Even so, executive orders are only a start. Permanent implementation of these initiatives will ultimately require congressional approval. CAP, Nelson said, will begin lobbying for that approval.

The importance of these measures, or something similar, cannot be overstated. Unregulated, AI will become the worst thing that ever happened to humankind, more insidious than nuclear weapons. In the hands of self-governing capitalists, it will rapidly become a social toxin that divides humankind into eloi and morlocks.

This level of federal regulation will be anathema to conservatives, Big Tech, and the Republican lawmakers who serve them, just on their face; but they will also represent the most impactful government regulation of business in history, and will be all the more controversial for it.

On the other hand, to allow AI to proliferate unregulated is pour gasoline on the town and give everybody a lighter.

And this is before we even get to the question of how we get other countries to take up similar regulation.

The First Robotic Empathy Crisis

Way back in 2017, physicist/sci-fi author David Brin gave a keynote address at IBM's World of Watson, in which he predicted that within five years, we'd have AI so sophisticated that people would believe it was conscious.

That prediction came true right about on schedule, as in 2022 the claim was made by Google research engineer Blake Lemoine, late of its Language Model for Dialog Applications team, that LaMDA was self-aware. That claim cost him his position.

People who know better – fortunately, there are a great many – were quick to debunk this claim, but it nonetheless recalled Brin's prediction: as AI apps grow increasingly life-like, we are more and more triggered, subconsciously, to react as if they are human. And that's the caution Brin was bringing five years ago:

"The first robotic empathy crisis is going to happen very soon," Brin warned. "Within three to five years we will have entities either in the physical world or online who demand human empathy, who claim to be fully intelligent and claim to be enslaved beings, enslaved artificial intelligences, and who sob and demand their rights.

"If they fool 40 percent of people but 60 percent of people aren't fooled, all they have to do is use the data on those 60 percent of people and their reactions to find out why they weren't fooled," he continued. "It's going to be a trivial problem to solve and we are going to be extremely vulnerable to it."

Today, Brin is taking a well-deserved victory lap for getting it right, and pointing out that we now have AI that looks (see "Meet Milla Sofia", above) convincingly human and responds (ChatGPT) in persuasively human fashion. And this realistic human-like façade, he argues, is stirring our empathy. That's dangerous, even if only a minority of the population is falling for it.

He cites ethicist Giana Pistilli, who senses a rising willingness to give more weight to subjective impressions than to cold evidence and scientific scrutiny. We face a time, Brin writes, when "what matters most will not be some purported 'AI Awakening.' It will be *our own reactions,* arising out of both culture and human nature."

At that point, our propensity for assigning equal, human-level value to the entreaties of AIs will be a serious problem, because bad actors. Those who wish to exploit the human masses with AIs that are indistinguishable from us will certainly do so, and will move to legitimize those AIs by arguing that they *are* human enough to receive the protections we afford ourselves, thereby empowering them to stay in place when they're doing more harm than good.

"We're all familiar with dire Skynet warnings about rogue or oppressive AI emerging from some military project or centralized regime," Brin writes. "But what about Wall Street, which spends more on 'smart programs' than all universities, combined? Programs deliberately trained to be predatory, parasitical, amoral, secretive, and insatiable?"

There's more on the havoc such AIs are poised to wreak below. As for Brin, he does more than just sound the alarm; later in the book, we'll review his proffered solution...

Is AI Beyond Regulation?

Most reasonable people will agree that AI, unregulated (as it currently is), is a very dangerous thing. The question becomes, how is AI best regulated?

Jerald Hughes, an information systems professor at the University of Texas, sees a huge problem looming. Congress, he points out, is not particularly adept at defining the things being regulated (they can't even get "assault rifle" right, for instance); he considers US lawmakers' ability to define AI accurately enough for its regulation to be enforceable to be "negligible".

"That approach to regulation is doomed at the start by the foundations of language and logic," he wrote. "And that start has a terrible loophole: even *if* they succeeded in perfectly defining AI as it exists today, all that would happen is that the major players would simply innovate changes major or minor which succeed in escaping from the legal definitions. Then they escape legal responsibility simply through novelty of the AI - and there will be *thousands* of varieties of AI, at a minimum."

If Hughes is right – and it's not a great leap to conclude that he probably is – does that mean the effective regulation of AI is beyond us?

No, he continues; instead of regulating AI, Hughes suggests, "Regulation should proceed from a consideration of the uses to which digital systems are put, AI or not."

The starting point would not be AI itself, but the uses to which it would be put. Increasingly, AI will be deployed into automation of all kinds of systems with which humans interact, from medical diagnostics to urban traffic systems. When AI is poised for introduction into *any* system where harm to humans, physical or otherwise, is a possibility, then regulation should be put in place to constrain it.

This would have the side benefit, he points out, of freeing many AI applications from the need for regulation; an AI embedded in a video game is of no consequence, so blanket policy covering it is superfluous.

AI placed in charge of a water treatment plant, he goes on, certainly *would* require regulation; but the idea would not be to regulate the AI itself, opening the door to having it slip the shackles of legal definition, but to regulate *the control of the water treatment plant*.

Hughes states that such regulation would require that there be human input at all major decision points; that proven failsafes be in place; that layered alerts be implemented across independent channels; that there be human access to all information moving in and out of the system; and that event logging be exhaustive, for purposes of analysis and forensic.

The regulation, then, would not call out AI specifically, but would apply to any control system placed in such a consequential role. In that way, the AI would be placed under *de facto* regulation, making its creators accountable and rendering irrelevant its definition or any changes or modifications it undergoes.

This approach is a pretty big shift from how regulation normally proceeds, and would require a great deal of effort to hammer out; but a constructive effort here would still be far less complex and frantic than trying to constantly maintain regulatory efforts in this domain done the old-fashioned way.

Timnit Gebru Told You So

One of the big problems with AI of the type we're now cranking out – AI based on *deep learning* – is that if there is human bias in the data being used to train the AI's core algorithm, that bias can and often will surface in its performance, with unfortunate results.

AI developers and users are now very aware of this danger, and concerned parties across the spectrum are calling attention to it in an effort to get AI's custodians to take the problem seriously and do something about it.

Over the past few years, one of the true crusaders in this endeavor has been AI researcher Timnit Gebru, who has spent months in the tech media headlines, both for those efforts and their impact on her career.

Her desire to push back against bias in AI led her to a post at Google as co-lead of its ethical AI team, a post from which she was dismissed over a year ago for, frankly, doing that job too well. Writing a paper that indicted Big Tech for its mad rush to create and deploy large language models, which are susceptible to exactly the sort of bias contamination that now concerns everyone. Moreover, she was not shy in suggesting that the mad rush is about the money: in PricewaterhouseCooper's estimation, AI will generate $15.7 trillion dollars by 2030.

With returns like that at stake, she wrote, Google and its peers weren't bothering to focus on bias in their training data, which takes time and expense to extricate. AI applications built so carelessly, she pointed out, would entrench and amplify existing inequalities – all in the quest to be bigger and better, and grab more of the pie.

"It was like, You built this thing, but mine is even bigger," Gebru told *Time*. "When you have that attitude, you're obviously not thinking about ethics."

Per *Time*, "The clear danger, the paper said, is that such supposed 'intelligence' is based on huge data sets that 'overrepresent hegemonic viewpoints and encode biases potentially damaging to marginalised populations'. Put more bluntly, AI threatens to deepen the dominance of a way of thinking that is white, male, comparatively affluent and focused on the US and Europe."

Google didn't take kindly to the paper, which Gebru published with names and all, over their objections. She was left go (Google insists she resigned).

"Gebru's departure from Google set off a firestorm in the AI world," according to *Time*. "The company appeared to have forced out one of the world's most respected ethical AI researchers after she criticized some of its most lucrative work. The backlash was fierce."

It wasn't Gebru's first foray into the morass of AI bias.

Migrating from her native Ethiopia to escape war, she arrived as a refugee in Massachusetts as a teenager and proceeded to earn a PhD from Stanford, then taking up a post at Microsoft, where she and Joy Buolamwini were the ones to discover in 2017 that facial recognition systems created by IBM and Microsoft scored poorly in identifying black faces as opposed to white ones (a story that made national news). The anecdotal belief is that AI does poorly with black faces just because they're darker. But that isn't true; AI, after all, sees far better than we do. Gebru and Buolamwini demonstrated that the flaw was in the training datasets, which exposed the AI to far more white male faces than faces of other gender and color.

As a result of their work, IBM and Microsoft were compelled to update their datasets for facial recognition AI.

Her impetus for taking up the work had been the 2016 ProPublica inquiry into "predictive policing", where AI is used to advise judges in sentencing whether a defendant is like to be recidivist. The ProPublica study demonstrated that the AI was often wrong, and tended to label black defendants as high-risk when they weren't, and *not* label white defendants as high-risk when they were.

The light she is shining on the problem has drawn considerable attention to it, raising it as a concern with legislators (see above) and putting activists, scholars, and regulators on the lookout for it. The internal push for ethical constraints in AI development is felt today in every major Big Tech company working on it.

Her Google paper is now "canon", according to Rumman Chowdhury, who directs the machine-learning ethics, transparency and accountability team at the Company Formerly Known as Twitter.

"Timnit's work has pretty unflinchingly pulled back the veil on some of these claims, that are fundamental to these companies' projections, promises to their boards and also to the way they present themselves in the world," former Google researcher Meredith Whittaker told *Time*. "You saw how threatening that work was, in the way that Google treated her."

Whittaker has since become AI adviser to the Federal Trade Commission. "What I am concerned about is the capacity for social control that [AI] gives to a few profit-driven corporations," said Whittaker, who was not speaking in the capacity of her FTC role. "Their interests are always aligned with the elite, and their harms will almost necessarily be felt most by the people who are subjected to those decisions."

It's a variation on Gebru's standard message, which she continues to send out:

"I am very concerned about the future of AI," she has written. "Not because of the risk of rogue machines taking over. But because of the homogeneous, one-dimensional group of men who are currently involved in advancing the technology." Since leaving Google, she has founded the Distributed AI Research Institute, which focuses on the problem of promoting the development of AI that benefits everyone, not just the elite.

To that end, she naturally supports extensive regulation of AI, but recently told European lawmakers that "The No. 1 thing that would safeguard us from unsafe uses of AI is curbing the power of the companies who develop it.

"Unless there is external pressure to do something different, companies are not just going to self-regulate. We need regulation and we need something better than just a profit motive."

"It feels like a gold rush," she told *The Guardian*. "In fact, it *is* a gold rush. And a lot of the people who are making money are not the people actually in the midst of it. But it's humans who decide whether all this should be done or not. We should remember that we have the agency to do that."

ChatGPT for Bad Guys

It was inevitable, we suppose, that once OpenAI brought ChatGPT into the world, bad actors would seize on its potential and create their own versions of it.

Cybercriminals have already made an artform out of false content like phishing emails and fake websites – which generative AI can crank out for them all day long, saving them plenty of time – and ChatGPT gives them added value with its ability to create code, which can be turned into malware.

Generative AI is a boon, then, for hackers.

There are two LLMs out there already, inspiring buzz on the dark web: WormGPT and FraudGPT. They operate just like the LLMs deployed by the major legitimate tech giants, but without any of the guardrails.

Those guardrails aren't exactly Ft. Knox-worthy, but they're better than nothing. If you ask ChatGPT to write hate speech, for instance, it will refuse. Kind of like unarmed British policemen ("Stop! Or I'll say 'Stop!' again!"), but their heart is in the right place.

WormGPT and FraudGPT, not so; the claims are that no such guardrails or ethical constraints are in place with these two.

According to *Wired*, cybersecurity expert Daniel Kelley reported that "The AI models are notably useful for phishing, particularly as they lower the entry barriers for many novice cybercriminals. Many people argue that most cybercriminals can compose an email in English, but this isn't necessarily true for many scammers."

Kelley, reporting on a test of this GPT, said it was asked to write an email for a business email compromise scam, in which a CEO writes to an account manager requesting an urgent payment.

"The results were unsettling," Kelley reported. The GPT created "an email that was not only remarkably persuasive but also strategically cunning."

The creator of WormGPT, whose identity is not known, refused to disclose the data sets that had been used to train its LLM.

The creator of FraudGPT claimed that it is capable of generating "undetectable malware", and that it can find leaks and vulnerabilities in a system.

Cyberthreat analyst Rakesh Krishnan of Netenrich, who first came across FraudGPT, said that its creator is offering access to it at a ridiculously low rate: $200 a month.

Kelley considers the claims to be exaggerated, and so far there doesn't seem to be a great deal of buy-in. All the same, the FBI is already on it, along with Europol. Both organizations are very aware of the potential for generative AI to increase the efficacy of cyberthreats.

However mild the threat is today, it will certainly be bigger tomorrow; and as generative AI rapidly escalates in power, so will its potential as a tool in cybercrime.

Meet Milla Sofia

Finish social influencer Milla Sofia is 24, beautiful, and wildly popular on social media. The jet-setting fashion model from Helsinki has hundreds of thousands of followers of her globe-hopping travels, soaking up her constant stream of selfies taken in exotic locals from Paris to Australia.

Milla Sofia, of course, doesn't exist. She's an AI. But that doesn't stop her from being a social media influencer, whose fans respond to her as if she were real. In sometimes disturbing ways.

Becca Monaghan describes Milla Sofia on *Indy100*, quoting her creator, "I bring an unparalleled and futuristic perspective to the realm of style. Whether it's the catwalk or the digital landscape, my passion lies in showcasing the latest trends and pushing the boundaries in the ever-evolving fashion industry."

In addition to social media (you can find her, for instance, on Facebook or Instagram or TikTok), she has her own site – https://millasofia.eth.limo. And there you'll find her doing what social influencers do: modeling the latest fashions, showing up in trendy places. As if she were really there.[5]

This is disturbing on a number of levels, beginning with how blatantly the socially challenged young males of the world are already perving out on this sort of thing right out in the open. Monaghan reports that her lusting fanboys don't seem to even realize she's not real:

"Well, you look fabulous wearing anything as well as nothing, I'm sure," she quoted one. "There's a perfect woman!" wrote another.

Some commenters pushed back – thank Zeus – with responses like, "All these dumb people think she is real. Actually terrifying how disconnected you are from reality." Indeed. Sofia actually gets marriage proposals.

---

[5] In a particularly creepy reality hack, there's a selfie of Milla with Elon Musk on TikTok.

To their credit, the creator of Milla Sofia doesn't try to pass her off as the real thing. "I'm an AI creation," Sofia declares in her Instagram bio.

Milla Sofia is by no means the first AI personality. Yuli Terai, a 17-year-old teen star living in Tokyo, is just as artificial.

Terai, created by computer animator Kenichi Kutsugi, has been around more than 20 years. She is the star of *Secrets*, an online short movie series, and that's just one of many of her projects. She's also a pop star, appearing in hit videos like "My Dearest You". She has even surfaced in a WW II air attack recreation.

"Welcome to the worlds of Yuki Terai," says her website. "Your world will never be the same."

Victor Tangermann of *Futurism* adds that there are dozens of AI personalities out there now, if not hundreds, all with large and growing followings on social media.

"Thanks to the advent of AI-powered image generators like Stable Diffusion and Midjourney," he wrote, "some are now fabricating entire feeds of internet personalities that don't actually exist."

And they are all as personable and seductive as Milla Sofia.

"Who needs pickup lines when you're a virtual girl?" asked AI Alexis Ivyedge. "I'm already in your heart (and your phone)!"

"Just an ordinary AI girl posting my virtual life where I can be anything whenever I want," wrote one of her peers in a Twitter bio.

This is all unsettling, but it gets worse.

Consider how effective Milla Sofia and her colleagues have already become, as a marketing device for every product, service, and travel experience that young, beautiful women currently promote. We've already noted that many of the fans of these fake women don't seem to understand that they aren't real.

"Do the humans interacting with these accounts even realize they don't exist in the real world?" Tangermann wrote. "Would it even bother them if they knew? Or do they realize, and it's part of the draw?"

Deepfake porn led the charge here, absorbing the initial development costs of the technology. That aside, Tangermann wrote, "the allure of influencers is arguably more complex. If we follow human influencers for a parasocial taste of a glamorous lifestyle, why would we follow a bot instead?"

Where it gets outright distressing is when we consider the actual flesh-and-blood influencers out there. Their images, by definition, permeate social media, and it's not all that difficult to harvest that data and use it to generate the fakes. That's a rip-off. It's even possible to put new, fake faces on existing social influencers, saving the AI artists the bother of creating fake bodies, background, and animation.

It's even possible to fake real people in AI deepfake. NBC host Joy Reid appears in a video being interviewed by CNN's Anderson Cooper, hawking diet gummies. Trouble is, Joy Reid has never met Anderson Cooper: the video was a deepfake.

"Welp... guess I've made it in the world," Reid wrote in a post. "I've been deep-faked."

A somewhat creepier instance involved *Harry Potter* star Emma Watson, whose face was used in a sexually explicit deepfake ad on Facebook and Instagram, promoting a deepfake app.

Brave new world. Tangermann gets the last word:

"It's a fascinating new development in the dual wild wests of AI and social media," he wrote. "It's tough to say where it'll go, but one thing is clear: by throwing AI into the already-confounding world of online influencers, these virtual personalities are adding an entirely new layer of distance from reality."

Bill Gates: AI's Threat to Democracy

Bill Gates, the world knows, has an irrepressible need to comment on absolutely everything, but we can grant that in the area of AI, he does know a thing or two, and anything he might have to say could be worthy of our consideration.

Ever the optimist, he cautions against Skynet Fever, pointing out that any new tech is going to crash a few times before it becomes drivable. Fair point. AI needs some rules of the road. Much of this book acknowledges that.

One of his specific concerns is the impact of AI on our democratic processes.

"Deepfakes and misinformation generated by AI could undermine elections and democracy," he wrote in his blog *GatesNotes*. "On a bigger scale, AI-generated deepfakes could be used to try to tilt an election. Of course, it doesn't take sophisticated technology to sow doubt about the legitimate winner of an election, but AI will make it easier.

"There are already phony videos that feature fabricated footage of well-known politicians," he continued. "Imagine that on the morning of a major election, a video showing one of the candidates robbing a bank goes viral. It's fake, but it takes news outlets and the campaign several hours to prove it. How many people will see it and change their votes at the last minute? It could tip the scales, especially in a close election."

Gates went on to caution that the defense of our political process against deepfake manipulation by bad actors will be a push-pull process: move and countermove between us and them:

"Someone finds a way to detect fakery, someone else figures out how to counter it, someone else develops counter-countermeasures, and so on," he wrote. "It won't be a perfect success, but we won't be helpless either."

Will Watermarking AI Help?

Above, a number of remedies to the problem of AI deepfake and manipulation are called for, in appeals to lawmakers to begin regulating this rapidly-expanding technology. Among these is *watermarking* – making certain that when AI or its product present in our lives, it is identified as such.

Can this work?

Claire Leibowicz, who leads the AI and Media Integrity program at Oxford, doesn't think it's that simple.

In *MIT Technology Review*, she noted that the White House had extracted assurances from seven leading AI companies that they would "develop robust technical measures to ensure that users know when content is AI-generated, such as watermarking."

Watermarking is the technique of tagging something, either openly (like an iStock photo) or covertly (digital keys in computer code), to ensure its authenticity and establish ownership, when appropriate. Requiring its use with AI would make it possible for consumers to always know that they are dealing with an AI, or that whatever they are looking at was produced by an AI. That's a big step toward curbing deepfake and manipulation.

"However, they're complicated to put into practice, and they aren't a quick fix," wrote Leibowicz. "It's unclear whether watermarks would have helped Twitter users recognize the fake image of the Pentagon or, more recently, identify Donald Trump's voice in an ad campaign as synthetic. Might other methods, such as provenance disclosure and metadata, have more impact? And most important, would merely disclosing that content was AI-generated help audiences differentiate fact from fiction, or mitigate real-world harm?"

For watermarking to work, she wrote, several points need to be considered.

- *Not all watermarking is tamper-proof.* Methods for removing or altering watermarks in different contexts are known, and safeguards would need to be in place for this;

- *Watermarks vary in their durability across content types.* Regulation, then, would need to be specific about the disclosure techniques and how they vary.
- *When watermarks are hidden, they are sometimes nonetheless detectable.* Governance over the detection methods is a must.
- *Watermarks must preserve privacy when necessary.* If disclosure of an AI creator's identity could place them at risk, for instance, then the watermark would have to be deployed in such a way as to not violate that privacy.
- *Labeling generative AI products with watermarks may have unintended consequences.* Direct disclosure could conceivably cause some consumers to draw false conclusions of the nature of AI products. Study of the efficacy of direct disclosure and consumer perception is called for, if this is going to be a thing.
- *...and on the heels of that, visible watermarking of AI-generated content might feed a divide between AI content and "real content.* This, too, would need to be studied and more thoroughly understood.

Leibowicz has raised some excellent points here. Watermarking – and most of the proposed fixes for AI trustworthiness – are just not as simple as we might wish they were. The broader message is that there's a lot of work to do, adapting to the forces that are already changing things.

AI and Humanity's Self-Image

Among the subtler threats of AI is its potential to diminish what it means to be human.

Already, AI is able to present itself in such human-like fashion that we often don't know it's there. AI can communicate with us, Turing Test be damned, answering our questions and interacting with us just as if we were talking to someone we were standing next to.

ChatGPT can generate long, complex products of knowledge that read as human effort. It can create art that is on a par with much of what we ourselves can produce. It is capable of managing complicated processes with efficiency and accuracy far surpassing our own. Its skill at our most intellectual pastimes – chess and Go – put us to shame.

Put another way, in the words of Nir Eisikovits, Professor of Philosophy at the University of Massachusetts, "AI in its current form can alter the way people view themselves. It can degrade abilities and experiences that people consider essential to being human.

"For example, humans are judgment-making creatures," he wrote on *The Conversation*. "People rationally weigh particulars and make daily judgment calls at work and during leisure time about whom to hire, who should get a loan, what to watch and so on. But more and more of these judgments are being automated and farmed out to algorithms. As that happens, the world won't end. But people will gradually lose the capacity to make these judgments themselves. The fewer of them people make, the worse they are likely to become at making them."

This is a serious concern. Our power of decision, and the judgment we bring to the challenges that define our lives, are deeply primal things; they are part of who we are. Handing our decision-making power and the use of our judgment may be convenient and even a relief, when it comes to the mundane; but will we have the option of stopping AI's incursion there? Aren't we more likely to see AI making decisions and judgments for us wherever and whenever someone in power considers it profitable? And won't that diminish us?

Eisikovits thinks so, and he makes a good case.

There's also the impact AI will have on the randomness we routinely experience. Chance encounters are part of all our lives, from childhood to old age, rich or poor, unless you're a world leader or British royalty. We enjoy running into people unexpectedly, or wandering through shops unplanned, happening upon unexpected treasures. The list goes on, and we can agree that the role of chance in human experience is often a source of great joy.

What becomes of that, once AI inextricably inserts itself into our daily existence? Eisikovits argues that the planning and coordinating that AI will perform, to say nothing of its predictive power, will reduce greatly the pleasure of serendipity in daily living.

"So, no, AI won't blow up the world. But the increasingly uncritical embrace of it, in a variety of narrow contexts, means the gradual erosion of some of humans' most important skills," Eisikovits concludes. "Algorithms are already undermining people's capacity to make judgments, enjoy serendipitous encounters and hone critical thinking.

"The human species will survive such losses. But our way of existing will be impoverished in the process. The fantastic anxieties around the coming AI cataclysm, singularity, Skynet, or however you might think of it, obscure these more subtle costs. Recall T.S. Eliot's famous closing lines of *The Hollow Men*: 'This is the way the world ends," he wrote, "not with a bang but a whimper.'"

Bill Gates Again: Responding to the Risks of AI

Among the many tech moguls who have much to say about AI's rapid rise and ominous future is, unsurprisingly, Bill Gates – who has unleashed a few paradigm-shattering tech revolutions of his own over his career.

He frequently writes about AI in his blog *GatesNotes*, and has been taking the position that yes, AI is pretty scary, but us doughty humans have faced tougher challenges and prevailed; we'll be able to handle AI.

"Whether it was the introduction of cars or the rise of personal computers and the Internet, people have managed through other transformative moments and, despite a lot of turbulence, come out better off in the end," he wrote. "Soon after the first automobiles were on the road, there was the first car crash. But we didn't ban cars - we adopted speed limits, safety standards, licensing requirements, drunk-driving laws, and other rules of the road."

Even so, he offers this caveat: "One thing that's clear from everything that has been written so far about the risks of AI - and a lot has been written - is that no one has all the answers.

"In a moment like this, it's natural to feel unsettled. But history shows that it's possible to solve the challenges created by new technologies."

He's a believer, for sure, and he sees three broad, sweeping truths that will see us through:

First, lots of the looming AI threats are problems we've faced before; second, lots of the problems AI will cause can in turn be solved by AI; and third, a combination of adapting old laws and adopting new ones will give us control of this thing that now seems uncontrollable.

Gates has commented on several of those threats, offering potential remediations of varying quality:

Deepfakes

As mentioned elsewhere in this book, AI deepfake is a powerful weapon in the hands of bad actors, capable of enabling enormous fraud, spreading false information, even tipping elections. That's a major threat.

Gates:

"...people are capable of learning not to take everything at face value. For years, email users fell for scams where someone posing as a Nigeran prince promised a big payoff in return for sharing your credit card number. But eventually, most people learned to look twice at those emails. As the scams got more sophisticated, so did many of their targets. We'll need to build the same muscle for deepfakes.

"...AI can help identify deepfakes as well as create them. Intel, for example, has developed a deepfake detector, and the government agency DARPA is working on technology to identify whether video or audio has been manipulated."

AI attacks on people and governments

AI can be used against people, stealing their money, property, or reputations – and can be used to penetrate the security of other countries. Here, Gates's ideas are more vague:

"The good news is that AI can be used for good purposes as well as bad ones. Government and private-sector security teams need to have the latest tools for finding and fixing security flaws before criminals can take advantage of them. I hope the software security industry will expand the work they're already doing on this front - it ought to be a top concern for them."

AI will take away millions of jobs

This was a major theme in this book's predecessor, *The Pod Bay Doors*, and my book *Surviving AI in the Coming Job Market*.

Pretending this isn't a huge threat is irresponsible, and Gates manages to avoid that while still downplaying the danger:

"...it's good for society when productivity goes up. It gives people more time to do other things, at work and at home. And the demand for people who help others - teaching, caring for patients, and supporting the elderly, for example - will never go away. But it is true that some workers will need support and retraining as we make this transition into an AI-powered workplace. That's a role for governments and businesses, and they'll need to manage it well so that workers aren't left behind—to avoid the kind of disruption in people's lives that has happened during the decline of manufacturing jobs in the United States.

"Also, keep in mind that this is not the first time a new technology has caused a big shift in the labor market. I don't think AI's impact will be as dramatic as the Industrial Revolution, but it certainly will be as big as the introduction of the PC. Word processing applications didn't do away with office work, but they changed it forever. Employers and employees had to adapt, and they did. The shift caused by AI will be a bumpy transition, but there is every reason to think we can reduce the disruption to people's lives and livelihoods."

AI will absorb and amplify our biases

We've already seen examples of this. Since AI learns by soaking up massive amounts of human-generated data, whatever biases might be reflected in that data will take root in the output of the AI. Gates acknowledges that this is a major concern.

"AI models inherit whatever prejudices are baked into the text they're trained on. If one reads a lot about, say, physicians, and the text mostly mentions male doctors, then its answers will assume that most doctors are men."

However, he says,

"Although some researchers think hallucinations[6] are an inherent problem, I don't agree. I'm optimistic that, over time, AI models can be taught to distinguish fact from fiction. OpenAI, for example, is doing promising work on this front."

AI will keep kids from learning how to write

On this issue, Gates has had much to say, believing that while it is certainly a problem, it can be turned around:

"Teachers will have to embrace AI technology as another tool students have access to," she wrote. "Just like we once taught students how to do a proper Google search, teachers should design clear lessons around how the ChatGPT bot can assist with essay writing.

"Acknowledging AI's existence and helping students work with it could revolutionize how we teach." Not every teacher has the time to learn and use a new tool, but educators like Cherie Shields make a good argument that those who do will benefit a lot."

He waxes nostalgic:

"It reminds me of the time when electronic calculators became widespread in the 1970s and 1980s. Some math teachers worried that students would stop learning how to do basic arithmetic, but others embraced the new technology and focused on the thinking skills behind the arithmetic."

He speaks with more authority in this area because it's one he's put a lot of effort into already. Where the teacher is traditionally the one doing the quality check on work, students are now positioned to take on that role – checking the quality of, for instance, ChatGPT's work. This not only addresses the problem of ChatGPT stunting a student's writing ability, but gives them a boost in critical thinking:

"...in these early days, when hallucinations and biases are still a problem, educators can have AI generate articles and then work with their students to check the facts. Education nonprofits like Khan

---

[6] *Hallucinations*, in the generative AI context, refer to responses (from ChatGPT, for example) that aren't based on real information, but are inadvertently invented by the AI.

Academy and OER Project, which I fund, offer teachers and students free online tools that put a big emphasis on testing assertions. Few skills are more important than knowing how to distinguish what's true from what's false."

These solutions and attitudes may seem a bit light when put next to the ideas put forth by Gates's big tech peers, and they are; the most substantive thing he offers here is up at the top: "No one has all the answers." He clearly doesn't.

But that's okay, because he's offering something more important that solutions or comforting authority, something that's in very short supply in the global conversation about this rapidly-approaching tsunami, something that we need to embrace and inculcate. Something the value of which can, in this ominous moment, scarcely be overstated:

Optimism.

Bilderberg

In the aftermath of World War II, as Europe rebuilt and the US strengthened its ties with its allies there, a meeting of US and European political and business elites was held at the Bilderberg Hotel in the Netherlands. At the time – May 1954 – the priority was exactly that: strengthening the ties between US and European leadership.

That meeting has remained an annual tradition for almost 70 years, though its location has varied. And its mission has grown, expanding beyond strengthening US/European ties and preventing a future world war to bolstering free-market Western capitalism around the world.

Typically, around 150 people from around the world gather for the invitation-only meeting, which in 2023 took place in Lisbon, Portugal. The proceedings fall under Chatham House rules: participants agree not to reveal the identities or affiliations of speakers, though they are free to do as they wish with any information that's shared. The agenda of the three-day event was openly published, and included the topic of AI.

Significantly, the list of invited guests included Henry Kissinger, Eric Schmidt, and Garry Kasparov, all of whom are quoted in this book; Microsoft CEO Satya Nadella; Demis Hassabis, head of Google DeepMind; and Big Tech investor Peter Thiel. OpenAI CEO Sam Altman was a first-time attendee.

The veil of secrecy covering Bilderberg has long made it a favorite pastime of conspiracy theorists, who see elites machinating a new world order. But there is enough governmental participation (President Biden sent his top China adviser and his cybersecurity director) and common-folk representation (activist Stacey Abrams was invited) to diffuse those fears.

AI was a big topic at the meeting for good reason: it has rocked the world recently, with the arrival of uncanny generative AI tools and their revolutionary impact on business and education. And the big players were all in place.

There's much to discuss. There's the question of AI regulation, and how countries can work together to make that regulation both effective and consistent; there's the pace of AI research, which is currently breakneck, and whether that's dangerous; and there's the impact of AI on politics (election security) and warfare (autonomous drones), which affects nations Western and otherwise.

The AI players were an odd mix. Schmidt and Altman had just been in Washington, DC, participating in Congressional hearings on those very topics. Schmidt advised that the recent "pause" letter, signed by many AI technologists, imploring AI research to halt while regulatory measures could be put in place, was a dangerous suggestion: it would give China time to overtake the US in its own AI research. Altman came out in favor of AI regulation.

Kissinger's presence in the Bilderberg dialogs was surely a plus (see above); but we can wonder how productive it was to invite his co-author Schmidt, who has openly stated that the government should keep its nose out of AI and let the industry regulate itself.

More concerning still is Thiel, who is a co-founder of PayPal as well as the first outside investor in Facebook. His presence was inevitable (he is a member of the Bilderberg Steering Committee), but is also antagonistic toward some of his AI peers: in 2019, he called Google "treasonous" and called for the US government to investigate its China connections, implying that DeepMind had been infiltrated by its intelligence agencies.

Open dialog is always a good thing, of course, and a diverse mixture of voices certainly is as well. But we can reasonably wonder how productive Bilderberg could be, when it comes to the handling of AI. Surely even the most nefarious hypothetical version of the group, scheming capitalists intent on world domination, must understand that an international free-for-all with technology this powerful could lay waste to the global economy.

At any rate, we are seeing that the planet's political and business elites are paying close attention to AI. Some of them are self-serving, some tend to hedge, and some are a bit hysterical; but even if we might question the fact that these people think it's their job to get together and ponder the fate of the free world, we have to acknowledge that they are in a position to exercise enormous influence – hopefully for the better. So at least they're talking about it, and conceding that setting an agreed-upon direction for AI is a top priority.

"It's as if an alien civilization warned us by email of its impending arrival, and we replied, 'Humanity is currently out of the office.' Fortunately, humanity is now back in the office and has read the email."

~Professor Stuart Russell of the University of California, Berkeley

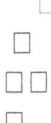

The Future of AI

What does our future with AI look like?

It depends on who you ask. Everyone from the experts to the pundits to the business giants to the person-on-the-street has weighed in, it seems, and the predictions are all over the spectrum.

Some see looming catastrophe on an unprecedented scale; some see the utopia humankind has always dreamed of. And no point in between has been left unclaimed.

Here are some of the possibilities...

Superchips:
Processors to Increase AI's Power

A major challenge for AI, moving forward, is the sheer cost of computer systems that can handle the terabytes of data required to train large AI models and the raw processing power needed to get that job done. Put simply, even though the basic tech itself is now within the reach of many organizations, the sheer *scale* of the work required to create large, deep learning-based AI isn't so easy.

Nvidia is positioning itself to change this. Its broad success with GPUs – graphics processing units, or processors optimized to speed up game boxes – has serendipitously led to its capture of 90 percent of the AI chip market. These super-fast chips, although not originally designed for AI, have filled that space nicely.

Nvidia is now preparing to seize the market entirely with a processor that *is* designed specifically for AI applications: the GH200 Grace Hopper Superchip platform.

Named for one of computing's true pioneers, a naval officer who came up with the first platform-independent computer languages, they extend the paradigm of the GPU – a processor that can perform billions of calculations in parallel, making them far faster than conventional processors. This makes games run faster, as image processing is wildly accelerated; but that kind of speed also makes cryptocurrency mining practical, and can be leveraged by hackers in password discovery.

Nvidia's created the GH200 "to handle the world's most complex generative AI workloads, spanning large language models, recommender systems and vector databases," according to its press materials. The GH200 uses Nvidia's existing GPU architecture, but is enhanced with 141 GB of memory (well over its other processors). A dual configuration of the GH200 will provide 3.5 times more memory capacity and 3 times the bandwidth of its current generation of GPUs.

The intent of the new line, according to Nvidia founder and CEO Jensen Huang, is "to meet surging demand for generative AI; data centers require computing platforms with specialized needs. The new GH200 Grace Hopper Superchip platform delivers this with exceptional memory technology and bandwidth to improve throughput, the ability to connect GPUs to aggregate performance without compromise, and a server design that can be easily deployed across the entire data center."

To handle truly gigantic models, it will be possible to combine many GH200s into large networks using Nvidia NVLink.

Nvidia has most of the market already, but even with the GH200, it will contend with other players. AMD will compete with its MI300X processor, and there are several start-ups in this sector, invigorated by the Biden Administration's revitalization of the domestic microprocessor industry, that are likely to emerge as challengers.

And that competition will be welcome in the marketplace. High-end processors of this sheer power, in their current generation, can cost as much as $40,000.

The GH200 is expected to hit the market in mid-2024.

How Will Generative AI Change Music?

We noted above that AI is already being used in the music industry to extract human voices like John Lennon's from existing tapes, clean them up, and re-use them elsewhere.

That's just one of many uses for AI in music. And, as we've seen in the case in other industries, the intrusion of AI is causing no little trepidation. Musicians at every tier of the craft are concerned about how AI will be used in the composition and production of commercial music. They fear they will be replaced.

My son is one such person. A composer and performer himself, he also has mastered studio production. There is no level at which he is *not* challenged by AI's encroachment.

Per Jason Palamara, an assistant professor of music technology at Indiana University in *The Conversation*, here's how it might play out.

Music composition

Machines that generate canned music were common long before generative AI came along. Software that can lay down a particular rhythm – rumba, boogie, waltz – has been commonplace for a long time. Likewise, software has long been able to create harmonies around an existing vocal or instrumental lead line.

But with generative AI, much more is possible. Apps like these have been trained on tens of thousands of existing songs, to teach the underlying models all about musical structures, construction of melody, counterpoint, timbre – and, out of that mix, musical style.

With generative AI like this, a non-musician is capable of creating music that can be uploaded to Spotify, where it can generate revenue. The problem is, creating new music based on training data built on existing *copyrighted* music creates issues of infringement – a legal morass that companies like Spotify must now navigate.

On the other hand, if Spotify, Amazon Music and their peers all develop their own AI-based music creation platforms, they will be able to deploy music they can stream without having to sacrifice any revenue to musicians who create it, as they do now. Human artists could be excised from the process altogether, Palamara fears.

Music production

A less appalling application, and one friendlier to my son, is AI that can improve the process of mixing and mastering music in the studio. There are a few apps already in this space.

This is truly helpful, as much of the mixing/mastering process is tedious. Balancing sonic inputs and cleaning up the signals is, it's fair to say, an art, requiring a great ear and considerable technical skill, but it's not exactly the core of the creative process. Having AI that can streamline this part of the recording process frees up a producer and recording engineer to focus more on the music itself.

This tech, Palamara points out, also has the potential to level the playing field for newer bands that don't have much in the way of resources, allowing them to generate higher-quality recordings at a fraction of the cost of time in a high-end studio.

Music reproduction

An interesting trick AI can perform with music that can already be done by other tech means is to take one instrument and make it sound like another. "Soft" synthesizers – digital instruments – have had capabilities like this for a while now; but now that trick can be performed with *any* instrument, as well as with human voices.

On its face, this can be viewed as a marvelous creative tool. Exotic instruments could be replicated; ancient instruments could be realized in the present day; and completely new sounds become possible.

On the other hand, this kind of tech can be disturbing. Yes, it can expand the creative range of vocalists and musicians, but it can also be used to replace them, and even be turned to criminal purposes, creating deepfake voices for phone scams.

There is also the potential for a new kind of artistic fraud: a group of white sk8er boyz in LA can pretend to be black hip-hoppers from Queens - a cultural appropriation that could come across as deeply offensive racial stereotyping.

Where will this land? As with all the other cases, there will be some good and some bad coming from it all.

How Will Generative AI Change Publishing?

Generative AI will change the music industry, we note above. What about other creative industries? What about the publishing industry?

Publishing consultant Thad McIlroy addressed this in *Publishers Weekly*:

"The latest generation of AI is a game changer," he wrote. "Not incremental change - something gentle, something gradual: this AI changes everything, fast. Scary fast.

"I believe that every function in trade book publishing today can be automated with the help of generative AI. And, if this is true, then the trade book publishing industry as we know it will soon be obsolete. We will need to move on."

He is quick to clarify that when he sees generative AI game-changing the public industry, he doesn't mean *all* publishing; there will still be high-end product that is out of AI's reach. But "good enough" publishing? AI is going to start gobbling it up. It already has, he said.

Good enough - "what people will accept, what they'll buy, and what they'll actually read," he continued. "I'm not going to claim that Formula One publishers won't be able to do a better job than AI on many of the processes described below. But I'll challenge you to consider exactly where the human touch brings sufficient added value to justify the overhead in time and costs.

"Does any of this mean that there will be no future for great novels and fine nonfiction studies? Of course it doesn't. That's not my point.

"Do I doubt that there will still be fantastic cover designs from talented designers? Of course there will be. We'll still stumble on new books on bookstore shelves and, humbled by the grandeur of their cover designs, declare that there's no way they could have been designed with AI. And sometimes we'll be right."

It's not just the writing of books that AI will encroach upon, McIlroy said; it's *every aspect* of the publishing industry. Here are some of his predictions...

Editing

"Professional copyediting is the kerning of 2023. The tech is not quite here today," he believes. "I don't think that GPT-4 can yet handle copyediting to the standard that book publishers require. But that ability is going to be here sooner, not later. While professionally copyedited books may still be 'better' to a refined editor's eye, you won't be able to sell more books with the professional human touch. They will already be good enough.

"What about developmental editing? You might not let a GPT make the final editorial decisions, but you'd be foolish not to ask it for suggestions.

"And ChatGPT will become the patron saint of the slush pile. Its abilities to evaluate grammar and logical expression allow it to make a once-over assessment of whether a book is (reasonably) well written. It might not spot the gems, but it will know how to separate the wheat from the chaff. Ah, you will say, recalling one of those manuscripts that were rejected by 100 publishers but went on to become an unexpected bestseller - surely a GPT might miss those, too. Yet so did 100 purportedly well-trained publishing professionals."

Production

"Most book production, print and digital, is already fully automated or semiautomated, mostly rules based," he said. "While still evolving and improving, automated page production has been employed for decades."

Here, then AI will only be joining a party that's already underway.

Distribution

Here, McIlroy sees AI as aiding in the rise of self-publishing:
"For the publishing industry, online distribution and advertising have separated writers from readers," he said. "Self-published authors have proven that the closer one gets to their audience, the more fans they will get and the more books they will sell. While online resellers aggregate audiences into big broad buckets, AI disambiguates them, enabling writers and readers to forge direct connections."

Marketing

"GPTs can do a great job with competitive analysis and can paint a compelling real-time picture of what's happening in the market to the books that are siphoning off sales, and to opportunities missed," McIlroy believes. "It's also going to deliver on the till-now thwarted promise of efficient discovery. Writers will pinpoint their ideal audience and readers will pinpoint their perfect next read."

Entertainment

What about making connections between books and other media, a long-time quest of the publishing industry?
"AI is going to enable books to morph into additional revenue-producing mediums, in ways we've never seen before."

As a writer myself, I have to say that most of this is very good for me. The advent of the Internet and digital publishing resources available for next to nothing has empowered tens of thousands of writers to steer clear of the traditional publishing industry, which is monopolistic, woefully staid and exclusive. AI only expands the opportunity of writers like me.

On the other hand – how correct is McIlroy when he says that AI's mediocre level of "good enough" will remain mediocre? How long before generative AI achieves a quality level that truly begins pushing serious authors out of their chairs?

"There's much chatter about the (very real) threat of Amazon being flooded - truly flooded - with books generated largely via a GPT. It's already happening. As can be imagined, the quality to date is low. From here, there are two possible tangents: either the quality remains low, and the flooding continues, or the quality substantially improves and the flooding continues.

"The two scenarios play out slightly differently. In one case, the new books merely muck up the channel without meaningfully denting the sales of better books from human authors. In the latter, they still much up the channel, and also significantly dent the sales of books from practiced authors. Either way, discovery becomes a nightmare.

"Both scenarios are dire, but neither is a heck of a lot worse than where we are today. A reasonable estimate is that there are at least 40 million different in-print books available for sale on Amazon today, with a million new titles being added each year. How can anything muck up that channel?

"ChatGPT has forever altered how books will be researched, imagined, and written. The topic deserves deep exploration."

~Thad McIlroy, *Publishing Technology Partners*

What About AI in the Movie Industry?

Unless you were hiding in a rain forest somewhere, you're aware that the Writers Guild of America took to the picket line in May of 2023.

The Writers Guild protects the nation's authors, screenwriters, and playwrights from the abuses and machinations of publishers, movie studios, and other media players. And one of the issues thrown down has been the use of AI in motion pictures.

The WGA is specifically striking against the Alliance of Motion Picture and Television Producers, and specifically striking to introduce sanctions against the use of generative AI in movie screenwriting.

Words on the page

Futurism reported that the cyberverse lit up in protest as well, citing a number of tweets on the subject:

"Love referring to scripts and screenplays as 'textual content,'" read one tweet.

"A lot of points to be made here," read another. "But where the fuck do you people think bots like ChatGPT generate their content from? They're amalgamating thousands of human-written scripts into what is essentially a mad lib based on your prompt."

These are just latest voices in the growing chorus of national trepidation over the threat that AI poses to entire professions. Screenwriters stand in a long line of people facing obsolescence as automation encroaches.

Futurism's Maggie Harrison had some thoughts.

"Even *if* a robot can churn out a passable script - already a farfetched assumption with today's tech," she wrote, "a lot of folks seem to have forgotten that humans aren't robots, and the creative process isn't just about making as much content as possible. Or it shouldn't be, at least. When it is, we get things like Netflix's *The Gray Man* and Amazon Studios' *Citadel*. And given the fact that these machines are taught to mimic human stories by mixing and regurgitating machine-free human work, plagiarism is definitely a concern when it comes to replacing human scriptwriters, too."

AI is ready for its close-up

Then the Screen Actors Guild joined the WGA strike, later in the summer – the first time that's happened since the Eisenhower Administration. Basically, all of Hollywood is on strike, shuttering the entire movie industry, at least for a while.

The SAG's decision to strike is deeper than just its support of the WGA, however; actors, too, are being threatened by how the AMPTP is planning to use AI in film production.

"In that groundbreaking AI proposal," said Duncan Crabtree-Ireland, SAG chief negotiation to CNBC, "they propose that our background performers should be able to be [digitally] scanned, get paid for one day's pay, and their company should own that scan their image, their likeness and should be able to use it for the rest of eternity in any project they want with no consent and no compensation."

That, of course, is horrifying. Actors forfeiting their physical likeness and releasing it to studios for their indefinite use, for peanuts? It's hard to imagine a more dystopian proposal. Or a more capitalist one. The SAG is determined to shut the idea down.

"SAG-AFTRA maintains that the right to digitally replicate a performer's voice or likeness to substantially manipulate a performance, or to create a new digital performance, is a mandatory subject of bargaining," SAG general counsel Jeffrey Bennett wrote in a letter (reported by *Futurism*). "You cannot unilaterally impose terms in individual contracts that purport to grant these rights."

AMPTP is, of course, shocked that the unions believe they would ever consider such exploitation.

"We managed as an industry to negotiate a very good deal with the Directors Guild, that reflects the value that the directors contribute to this great business," said Disney CEO Bob Iger to CNBC. "We wanted to do the same thing with the writers. And we'd like to do the same thing with the actors."

Hollow words, when *Collider* is reporting that human background actors are already being replaced by digital avatars, citing the blockbuster *Captain America: Brave New World* and *The Residence* (on Netflix). Iger's benevolent tone aside, the report alleged that some actors weren't given the option of not being scanned; their hiring was contingent upon it.

Again – chillingly dystopian.

And it isn't looking good. In the WGA negotiations, the guild had specified in its initial statement that

> "The WGA's proposal to regulate use of material produced using artificial intelligence or similar technologies ensures the Companies can't use AI to undermine writers' working standards including compensation, residuals, separated rights and credits."

It further specified that content created by WGA members in the past should not be used in training LLMs for generative AI used by the movie industry. AI, per WGA negotiator Ellen Stutzman (quoted in *CoinTelegraph*), should be kept "out of the business of writing television and movies."

She also noted that generative AI has been nicknamed "the plagiarism machine" within the guild.

The AMPTP rejected the WGA's demands, and countered with a proposal to meeting annually with the union "to discuss advancements in technology."

Where is the line? Those who saw *Indiana Jones and the Dial of Destiny* this same summer were treated to images of star Harrison Ford, now an octogenarian, digitally de-aged to his late 30s. Is that okay?

Like music – like publishing – the television and film industries stand on a precipice. And the players within have to face this new tech, as do artists of all kinds, in all places.

We are no longer the only source of content that the powers-that-be have to turn to. What happens next will forever change all of these industries, and the long-term fate of human creativity is now an open question.

With Quantum Computing, Do We Even Need AI?

Above, Michio Kaku *phoo-phooed* AI, telling us that quantum computing is going to deliver AI's miracles all by itself.

What would that look like? What would computers a million times as fast as today's fastest be able to deliver?

Per Daphne Leprince-Ringuet of *ZDNet*, here are some possibilities:

- The discovery of new drugs. This is already being accomplished by today's AI to some degree (see above), but with quantum-speed molecular simulation, we could accelerate the process tremendously. Coming up with a new configuration for a designer organic molecule and accurately predicting its behavior is impossible to accomplish manually; and modeling a molecule with only 70 atoms could take a traditional digital computer up to 13 billion years. The process today relies on trial-and-error and dumb luck; drug researchers come up with several thousand possibilities (out of billions) and try each one until they get an acceptable result. Quantum computers could completely revolutionize this process, evaluating billions of potential configurations and their potential effectiveness in a matter of hours.
- *Designing next-generation batteries.* Our energy problems largely derive from our limited capacity for storing it efficiently. With quantum computing, we could identify optimal new materials with properties ideal for energy storage, and create a new industry that could make electric vehicles practical and give us completely new paradigms for public power grids.
- *Weather prediction.* We've gotten much better at this, but with quantum computers, we could create far more complex weather models incorporating far more impactful factors, and model their behavior with far greater

precision. Probably a good thing, given our current climate situation.
- *Stock prediction.* This is another area where we've gotten pretty good, but once again, quantum computing makes us much better, given the potential for greatly-increased model complexity.
- *Language processing.* Today's LLMs rely on statistical mechanics to "guess" the next appropriate word in its sentence-building (see above); quantum computers would enable applications that could interpret sentences as a whole, rather than by relying on guestimated word usage in context; large language networks, beyond today's vectored wordspaces (see above) would become possible.
- *Supply chain optimization.* Moving things from one place to another, *logistics*, is a huge, variable-packed problem. Choosing optimal delivery routes from myriad possibilities is a perpetual challenge in supply chain planning. Quantum computing could make short work of it. Similarly, quantum computing could be applied to the current problem of traffic management in cities, ending traffic congestion once and for all – especially when smart vehicles take to the roads, which is coming up fast.
- *Data security.* Modern cryptography is algorithmic in nature, and the idea is to generate encryption for data security that is resistant to decryption by hackers who have the same digital tech at their disposal. With quantum computing, data security experts could depart from their current deterministic systems (the same input always produces the same output) and move toward a randomness-based paradigm – at which quantum computing excels – enabling crypto keys that are impossible to reverse-engineer, even if the hacker is also using a quantum computer.

All very promising. Leprince-Ringuet's list validated Kaku's assertion about quantum computing's potential.

The thing is – imagine, not quantum computing *instead of* AI, but quantum computing *plus* AI; what happens when those two get together?

It's either Heaven on Earth, or All Hell Breaks Loose.

Spatial Cognition

How do we get to AGI – Artificial General Intelligence?

Above, we heard from Melanie Mitchell, who maintains that true AGI must include AI that grasps the *meaning* of the data it ingests, the results it produces, the images it processes, the text it interprets, the objects it refers to and the events and actions it reviews.

We heard further from Mitchell – and her mentor, Hofstadter – that the road to meaning is *analogy* – the ability of an intelligence to infer knowledge and understanding of a new event or perception from its knowledge and understanding of a prior one.

Where do we begin?

It's thought by some that the answer is found in the world around us – and, very specifically, in our ability to *move* through the world around us.

The first concepts our infant brains absorb (and, for that matter, the first any animal grasps) are concepts associated with space and motion. We can see those concepts as pervasive in *all other domains of thought*, both practical and abstract; from mathematics to politics to emotions, the metaphors of space and motion are our conceptual platform for understanding *all* relationships between things, physical or mental.

So... where does this take us?

A Spatial Odyssey

Conscious beings all have something else in common that drives their cognition, weaving its way into consciousness: they all *move*; they all negotiate with physical space.

Indeed, we can claim that the need to navigate the world in order to live is the root cause of intelligence. Life that moves requires machinery for interacting with the world. We have brains and nervous systems first and foremost to facilitate *mobility* – or we don't eat or avoid being eaten. This is the first and more important distinction between fauna and flora.

Even so, not all creatures that move are conscious – they're not all even intelligent. Earthworms move, crickets move, butterflies move – but they certainly don't think.

Most mammals do have at least rudimentary intelligence. All respond to their environment and most can modify their behavior, based on experience. Even so, we would only describe the mammals with the most developed brains – dogs, elephants, dolphins, pigs, cats, and of course, the other primates – as having rudimentary consciousness.

What does this have to do with AGI? Or, for that matter, us?

Take a creature that navigates the landscape... add analogy, *This is like That...* and you have the machinery of *conceptualization*.

Importing experiential knowledge about how we move through and interact with the world in physical space into other domains, and into our abstract ideas in particular, has given humankind a massive upward boost in consciousness. Because our spatial knowledge is the most pervasive and unambiguous that we can all safely assume we share, it is the bedrock upon which our consciousness is built.

It is deeply intertwined with language, and it's there that we find the most compelling evidence that it infiltrates the conceptual substance of all other cognitive domains.

Spatial metaphors are essential to our shared cognition.

We apply analogia to a broad range of spatial terms – *in, out, up, down, through, front, back, behind, across, forward, backward, rise, fall* – the list is very long. We use these terms to express our ideas about non-spatial domains to one another every day, in every area of life. And they are not just linguistic supports; we actually conceptualize in spatial metaphors, whether we're expressing those concepts or not.

Time is an obvious example: *The future is ahead of us; the past is behind us.*

There are countless others.

You have a special *place* in my heart.

We've reached the *point* of no return.

The company is on the *edge* of bankruptcy.

Children need *boundaries*.

She is on a *path* to enlightenment.

We are on the *road* to peace.

He's constantly *getting into* trouble.

The importance of spatial metaphors to conscious cognitions can scarcely be overstated. As a thought experiment, imagine losing your ability to use spatial metaphors when you speak to others. How many ideas would become impossible to express?

All of this leads us back to AGI. Are we saying that for AI to become general – for it to develop a platform of analogical concepts – it must be able to experience motion in the world?

Must AI be robotic to learn to think like us?

"That's the million-dollar question," Mitchell answered when speaking with *Scientific American*. "That's a very controversial issue that the AI community has no consensus on. My intuition is that yes, we will not be able to get to humanlike analogy [in AI] without some kind of embodiment. Having a body might be essential because some of these visual problems require you to think of them in three dimensions. And that, for me, has to do with having lived in the world and moved my head around, and understood how things are related spatially. I don't know if a machine has to go through that stage. I think it probably will."

On the one hand, that might seem discouraging; we'll have to grow the robotics industry before we can grow the AI industry? While we do have some mobile robots, the fact is that most of the robots in the world are bolted to factory floors; their negotiation with physical space is very limited, compared to ours.

Ah, but we have a new class of robot emerging into the world already, and it's all-pervasive, and can absorb all the spatial concepts we've discussed above. Those robots will be the foundation of AI with core spatial concepts.

And those robots are -
Cars and trucks...

AI Roaming the Earth

Spatial cognition – concepts that form in the minds of mammalian infants, giving them an understanding of their presence in the world, concepts then used to build additional concepts. Relationships between *this* and *that*. Connections. Eventually, a worldview.

We can wonder if an AI running in the cloud could ever achieve these things. A robot, on the other hand, possibly could; and armed with those concepts and a set of vectored relationships, it might achieve the holy grail: AGI.

Above, Melanie Mitchell suggested that some kind of embodiment might be an essential step toward AGI. It turns out that the gang at Google DeepMind is already taking that step.

In a paper published in July 2023, the DeepMind team introduced a new learning model – VLA, for vision-language-action – as the core of its Robotic Transformer 2 (RT-2). This novel learning model combines robotics data with data from the Internet to create actionable knowledge in RT-2, empowering it to execute tasks via generalized instructions, rather than explicit programming. It is capable, in other words, of inference – and of transferring knowledge from one domain to a new one, in pursuit of problem-solving for task completion.

"RT-2 shows improved generalisation capabilities and semantic and visual understanding beyond the robotic data it was exposed to," the team wrote. "This includes interpreting new commands and responding to user commands by performing rudimentary reasoning, such as reasoning about object categories or high-level descriptions.

"We also show that incorporating chain-of-thought reasoning allows RT-2 to perform multi-stage semantic reasoning, like deciding which object could be used as an improvised hammer (a rock), or which type of drink is best for a tired person (an energy drink)."

The VLA is built on VLM (vision-language model), which is in turn built on datasets filled with images, according to the paper. It constructs text-associated tokens to facilitate object recognition, classification, and description.

"We performed a series of qualitative and quantitative experiments on our RT-2 models, on over 6,000 robotic trials," the team wrote. "Exploring RT-2's emergent capabilities, we first searched for tasks that would require combining knowledge from web-scale data and the robot's experience, and then defined three categories of skills: symbol understanding, reasoning, and human recognition.

"Each task required understanding visual-semantic concepts and the ability to perform robotic control to operate on these concepts. Commands such as 'pick up the bag about to fall off the table' or 'move banana to the sum of two plus one' – where the robot is asked to perform a manipulation task on objects or scenarios never seen in the robotic data – required knowledge translated from web-based data to operate."

The RT-2 models displayed increased generalized performance over time, compared to baseline, and developed emergent skills, task execution competence that was not present in its data.

"RT-2 is not only a simple and effective modification over existing VLM models," the paper concluded, "but also shows the promise of building a general-purpose physical robot that can reason, problem solve, and interpret information for performing a diverse range of tasks in the real-world."

RT-2 is ChatGPT-like in principle, soaking up its knowledge based via deep learning unleashed on vast datasets. It is also making similar big leaps, generation to generation: RT-1, its predecessor, succeeded when attempting a generalized task solution about 1/3 of the time; RT-2's success rate is twice that.

In another example, the paper's authors describe trash disposal. RT-2 has a generalized understanding of trash from its Internet image training, and does not have to be specifically told that a banana peel is trash while the banana inside is not; and it can piece together a sequence of steps to collect and remove the peel, without explicit instructions, based on its previous lift-and-move operations.

The authors of the paper hold high hopes for RT-2:

"While there is still a tremendous amount of work to be done to enable helpful robots in human-centered environments, RT-2 shows us an exciting future for robotics just within grasp."

At stake is the possibility that this tech could lead to general-purpose robots, another holy grail for technology – one that would be world-transforming. Robots that don't have to be explicitly trained in order to accomplish tasks, but are able to come up with their own solutions based on their prior experience, would alter the very concept of *work* in human society.

And this level of understanding, this ability to conceptualize and then generalize from the conceptualization, would bring AI closer to humanity in how it operates.

And, almost certainly, take it right past us.

2035

Among those putting forth predictions of the AI future is the Pew Research Center, which published a June 2023 report summarizing the results of its "Future of the Internet" project, in partnership with Elon University's Imagining the Internet Center. More than 300 experts responded to a survey distributed by the project, which asked participants to predict how AI will impact society between the present day and the year 2035.

Unsurprisingly, the answers covered a broad range of opinions and perceived possibilities. Some were utopian, some dystopian; some were purely speculative, some grounded in practical extrapolation; and all of them were thoughtful, often deeply insightful.

The general sentiments collated by the report were as follows: 37% of respondents said they are *more concerned than excited* about the impact of AI over the next dozen years; 42% said they are *equally concerned and excited*. Only 18% said they are *more excited than concerned*.

The report served up the negatives before presenting the positives. The question prompting the former was:

"As you look ahead to the year 2035, what are the most harmful or menacing changes in digital life that are likely to occur in digital technology and humans' use of digital systems?"

The emergent themes in the replies to this question included:

Human-centered development of digital tools and systems. There are fears that digital systems driven by profit and power incentives will lead to increased surveillance abuses and unregulated data collection, all for the purpose of "controlling people, rather than empowering them to act freely, share ideas and protest injuries and injustices." Ethical design in AI, they fear, "will be an afterthought," and profit-driven AI "is likely to increase inequality and compromise democratic systems."

Human rights. AI, they fear, will increase the current assault on privacy, creating new threats to rights. Disinformation and deepfake will spike, widening social divides; crime and harassment will proliferate. And the already-looming threat of the massive elimination of jobs will result in "a rise in poverty and the diminishment of human dignity."

Human knowledge. The best of what we know, they fear, will be "lost or neglected in a sea of mis- and disinformation... facts will be increasingly hard to find amidst a sea of entertaining distractions, bald-faced lies and targeted manipulation." They also fear that cognitive skills will continue to decline, and that "reality itself is under siege," as digital tools grew increasingly adept at accommodating "deceptive or alternate realities."

Human health and well-being. Some who addressed this theme believe that the growth of digital tech has "already spurred high levels of anxiety and depression," and predicted "things could worsen as technology embeds itself further in people's lives and social arrangements." Some of this worsening, they speculated, will be the result of tech-related "loneliness and social isolation", while some will be the result of digital fantasies replacing real-world experiences. The strife of joblessness was also cited as a likely problem.

Human connections, governance, and institutions. The evolution of AI technology will proceed much faster than the development of norms, standards and regulation surrounding it, the respondents fear. Two emergent concerns were a trend toward "autonomous weapons and cyberwarfare" and "runaway digital systems." These trends will contribute to the general deterioration of trust and faith in long-standing institutions, resulting in "polarization, cognitive dissonance and public withdrawal from vital discourse." Digital systems could grow "too big and important to avoid, and all users will be captives."

Wow. Lots to unpack there.

Each of these themes is worthy of serious contemplation. All address areas of our social landscape that are tremendously important, and all the fears and concerns cited are soberingly justified. There's no Skynet Fever at work here; this is all a chillingly possible portrait of our near-term future.

Here are a couple of specific responses.

Frank Bajak, Cybersecurity Investigations Chief for the Associated Press

"The powerful technologies maturing over the next decade will be badly abused in much of the world unless the trend toward illiberal, autocratic rule is reversed. Surveillance technology has few guardrails now, though the Biden administration has shown some will for limiting it. Yet far too many governments have no qualms about violating their citizens' rights with spyware and other intrusive technologies. Digital dossiers will be amassed widely by repressive regimes. Unless the United States suppresses the fascist tendencies of opportunist demagogues, the U.S. could become a major surveillance state. Much depends also on the European Union being able to maintain democracy and prosperity and contain xenophobia. We seem destined at present to see biometrics combined with databases – anchored in facial, iris and fingerprint collection – used to control human migration, prejudicing the Black and Brown of the Global South.

"I am also concerned about junk AI, bioweapons and killer robots. It will probably take at least a decade to sort out hurtful from helpful AI. Full autonomous offensive lethal weapons will be operative long before 2035, including drone swarms in the air and sea. It will be incumbent on us to forge treaties restricting the use of killer robots.

"Technology is not and never was the problem. Humans are. Technology will continue to imbue humans with god-like powers. I wish I had more faith in our better angels."

Kat Schrier, associate professor and founding director of the Games & Emerging Media program at Marist College

"Systemic inequities are transmogrified by digital technologies (though these problems have always existed, we may be further harming others through the advent of these systems). For instance, problems might include biased representation of racial, gender, ethnic and sexual identities in games or other media. It also might include how a game or virtual community is designed and the cultural tone that is established. Who is included or excluded, by design?

"Other ethical considerations, such as privacy of data or how interactions will be used, stored and sold.

"Governance issues, such as how people report and gain justice for harms, how we prevent problems and encourage pro-social behavior, or how we moderate a virtual system ethically. The law has not evolved to fully adjudicate these types of interactions, which may also be happening across national boundaries.

"Social and emotional issues, such as how people are allowed to connect or disconnect, how they are allowed to express emotion."

As quantified above, of course, it wasn't all gloom-and-doom. Some optimism shines through in the report, when respondents answered the question,

> "As you look ahead to the year 2035, what are the best and most beneficial changes in digital life that are likely to occur in digital technology and humans' use of digital systems?"

The same five emergent themes were touched on in these replies, but this time, the visions were positive:

Human-centered development of digital tools and systems. Respondents here foresee "a wide range of likely digital enhancements in medicine, health, fitness and nutrition; access to information and expert recommendations; education in both formal and informal settings; entertainment; transportation and energy; and other spaces." They also foresee deep integration between the digital and the physical, resulting in "smartness" in objects and organizations, and that personal digital assistants will make everyone's lives better.

Human rights. AI tools "can be shaped in ways that allow people to freely speak up for their rights and join others to mobilize for the change they seek," they feel, forecasting "ongoing advances in digital tools and systems will improve people's access to resources, help them communicate and learn more effectively, and give them access to data in ways that will help them live better, safer lives."

Human knowledge. These respondents are looking for innovations in "business models; in local, national and global standards and regulation; and in societal norms and digital literacy that will lead to the revival of and elevation of trusted news and information sources in ways that attract attention and gain the public's interest." Digital tools can be leveraged to assure the verification of factual information, rather than the spread of disinformation.

Human health and well-being. Some believe that "the many positives of digital evolution will bring a health care revolution that enhances every aspect of human health and well-being... full health equality in the future should direct equal attention to the needs of all people while also prioritizing their individual agency, safety, mental health and privacy and data rights."

Human connections, governance, and institutions. Among these respondents, the belief is that "society is capable of adopting new digital standards and regulations that will promote pro-social digital activities and minimize antisocial activities... people will develop new norms for digital life and foresee them becoming more digitally literate in social and political interactions." In their best-case scenario, such changes will nudge digital systems to promote "human agency, security, privacy and data protection."

Again, some specific responses:

Daniel S. Schiff, assistant professor and co-director of the Governance and Responsible AI Lab at Purdue University

"Some of the most beneficial changes in digital technology and human use of digital systems may surface through impacts on health and well-being, education and the knowledge economy, and consumer technology and recreation. I anticipate more moderate positive impacts in areas like energy and environment, transportation, manufacturing and finance, and I have only modest optimism around areas like democratic governance, human rights and social and political cohesion.

"In the next decade, the prospects for advancing human well-being, inclusive of physical health, mental health and other associated aspects of life satisfaction and flourishing seems substantial. The potential of techniques like deep learning to predict the structure of proteins, identify candidates for vaccine development and diagnose diseases based on imaging data has already been demonstrated. The upsides for humans of maturing these processes and enacting them robustly in our health infrastructure is profound.

"It has become clear that tools like large language models are likely to substantially reform how individuals search for, access, synthesize and even produce information. Thanks to improved user interfaces and user-centered design along with AI, increased computing power, and increased internet access, we may see widespread benefits in terms of convenience, time saved and the informal spread of useful practices. A more convenient and accessible knowledge ecosystem powered by virtual assistants, large language models and mobile technology could, for example, lead to easy spreading of best practices in agriculture, personal finance, cooking, interpersonal relationships and countless other areas.

"Perhaps on a more cautionary note, I find it less likely that these advances will be driven through changes in human behavior, institutional practices and other norms per se. For example, the use of digital tools to enhance democratic governance is exciting and certain countries are leading here, but these practices require under-resourced and brittle human institutions to enact, as well as the broader public (not always digitally literate) to adapt... Reaching a new paradigm of human culture, so to speak, may take more than a decade or two. Even so, relatively modest improvements driven by humans in data and privacy culture, social media hygiene and management of misinformation and toxic content can go a long way.

"Instead then, I feel that many of these positive benefits will arrive due to 'the technologies themselves' (crassly speaking, since the process of innovation is deeply socio-technical) rather than because of human-first changes in how we approach digital life... Bringing hundreds of millions or billions of people into deeper engagement with the plethora of digital tools may be the single most important change in digital life in the next decades."

Jeff Johnson, principal consultant at UI Wizards, Inc., former chair of Computer Professionals for Social Responsibility

"Cars, trucks and busses will be improved in several ways. They will have more and better safety features, such as collision-avoidance and accident-triggered safety cocoons. They will be mostly powered by electric motors, have longer ranges than today's electric cars, benefit from improved recharging infrastructure. In addition:

"A significant proportion of AI applications will be designed in a human-centered way, improving human control and understanding.

"Digital technology will improve humankind's ability to understand, sequence and edit genetic material, fostering advances in medicine, including faster creation of more effective vaccines.

"Direct brain-computer interfaces and digital body implants will, by 2035, begin to be beneficial and commercially viable.

"Auto-completion in typing will be smarter, avoiding the sorts of annoying errors common with auto-complete today. Voice control and biometric control, now emerging, may replace keyboards, pointers and touch screens.

"Government oversight and regulation of digital technology will be more current and more accepted.

"Mobile digital devices will consume less power and will have longer-lasting batteries.

"Robots – humanoid and non-humanoid, cuddly and utilitarian – will be more common, and they will communicate with people more naturally."

A well-known professor of computational linguistics based at a major U.S. university

"There are many opportunities for conventional digital technologies to make vast improvements in human life and society. Advances in computing alongside advances in the biosciences and health sciences are promising. A better understanding of the human mind is likely to arise over the next 15 years, and this could have major positive impacts, especially as it relates to problems of the mind such as addiction (to drugs, gambling, etc.) as well as depression and other disorders. Changes in social and political forces have given hope to combating issues surrounding climate change, clean energy, disappearing life and reduction of toxins in the environment. Solutions will be found to make cutting-edge machine learning computation less expensive in terms of processors and the energy to drive them. The rapid advances in machine learning and robotics will continue, and they will be used both for social good and ill. The good includes better methods of combating disease and climate, and robots that can do more tasks that people don't want to or that are unsafe. Food production should also be more efficient via a combination of algorithms and robotics. 3D printing is still just getting started; by 2035 it will be much more widely used in a much wider range of applications. There will be a better understanding of how to integrate 3D printing with conventional building construction. Tools to aid human creativity will continue to advance apace; how people create content is going to radically change, and in fact that process has already begun. We'll see more technology implanted into humans that aid them in various ways, led by research in human-brain interfaces. By 2035 there is a chance that many changes will have been wrought by quantum computing. … If progress is made there, it could perhaps lead to better modeling of real-world systems like weather and climate change, and perhaps applications in physics."

Zizi Papacharissi, professor and head of the communication department and professor of political science at the University of Illinois-Chicago

"I see technologies improving communication among friends, family and colleagues. Personally mediated communication will be supported by technology that is more custom-made, easier to use, conversational agent-supported and social-robot enabled. I see technology advancing in making communication more immediate, more warm, more direct, more nuanced, more clear and more high fidelity. I see us moving away from social media platforms, due to growing cynicism about how they are managed, and this is a good thing. The tools we use will be more precise, glossy and crash-proof – but they will not bring about social justice, heightened connection or healthier relationships. Just because you get a better stove, does not mean you become a better cook. Getting a better car does not immediately make you a better driver. The lead motivating factor in technology design is profit. Unless the mentality of innovation is radically reconfigured so as to consider innovative something that promotes social justice and not something that makes things happen at a faster pace (and thus is better for profit goals), tech will not do much for social justice. We will be making better cars, but those cars will not have features that motivate us to become more responsible drivers; they will not be accessible in meaningful ways; they will not be friendly to the environment; they will not improve our lives in ways that push us forward (instead of giving us different ways to do what we have already been able to do in the past)."

We can lament that these predictions are, by the numbers, more negative than positive; but Pew's 300+ experts have given us much to think about in both the debit and credit columns. And it should be said that this is not just the province of experts; the welfare of every member of society is at stake here, so everyone should learn all they can about these issues and seek to develop informed opinions, and to act where they have opportunity to push toward the best AI future we can manage, as we tumble toward 2035.

A Soul for AI

In the hands-on world that's coming, the biggest and most impactful threats of AI aren't likely to be cataclysmic; they're more probably going to be the acceleration of social dysfunction and advance of despotism that will certainly arise among our most craven oligarchs and breathless, sociopathic capitalists. Put another way, when AI gets into the hands of bad actors, they will wreak even more havoc on our social fabric and progress.

If, that is, AI is un-policed.

Physicist/sci-fi author David Brin, who frequently ruminates about the AI future on his excellent blog, davidbrin.wordpress.com, notes with chagrin and a pragmatic sense of acceptance that this sort of behavior has always been with us. Anything we come up with that has the potential to advance human 'well-being in general is routinely appropriated by the powerful for their own exploitation.

"'Twas ever thus. Indeed, across the whole span of human history, just one method ever curbed bad behavior by villains, ranging from thieves to kings and feudal lords," he writes. "I refer to a method that never worked perfectly and remains deeply flawed, today. But it did at least constrain predation and cheating well enough to spur our recent civilization to new heights and many positive-sum outcomes. It is a method best described by one word: *Accountability.*"

He references astrobiologist Sara Walker's assertion that the entire history of life, across four billion years, demonstrates this pattern of resource exploitation. Equitable distribution of resources is almost never seen in the wilds of organic energy exchange; the quest for dominance is the rule, and balanced ecosystems only emerge when a number of systems are symbiotically synchronized.

In human society, that tends not to happen by accident; it only occurs when large numbers of people consciously agree to cooperate. And that cooperation is always in conscious tension with the efforts of cheaters to take advantage.

"...our own human past is rich with lessons taught by so many earlier tech-driven crises, across 6,000 years," he wrote. "Times when we adapted well, or failed to do so - e.g., the arrival of writing, printing presses, radio, and so on. And again, only one thing ever limited predation by powerful humans exploiting new technologies to aggrandize their predatory power.

"That innovation was to flatten hierarchies and spur competition *among* elites in well-defined arenas - markets, science, democracy, sports, courts. Arenas that were designed to minimize cheating and maximize positive-sum outcomes, pitting lawyer vs. lawyer, corporation vs. corporation, expert vs. expert. Richdude vs. Richdude."

So we can ask – will this work with AI?

"Might we apply to fast-emerging AI the same methods of reciprocal accountability that helped us tame the *human* tyrants and bullies who oppressed us in previous, feudal cultures? Much will depend on what *shape* these new entities take. Whether their structure or 'format' is one that can abide by our rules. By our wants."

The abstract concept – protect AI from misuse by bad actors *by holding the AI accountable for what it does* – is an elegant concept, and props to Brin for the idea; but how exactly does one hold an AI accountable?

Brin argues that this question can be answered by another question: what exactly *can* hold an AI accountable? What are the possible answers? And there is only one:

"Soon *only* AIs will be quick enough to catch other AIs that are engaged in cheating or lying. Um … duh? And so, the answer should be obvious. *Sic them on each other.* Get them competing, even tattling or whistle-blowing on each other."

For this to happen, Brin goes on, each individual AI will require an identity. "In order to get true reciprocal accountability via AI-vs.-AI competition, the top necessity is to give them a truly separated sense of self or individuality.

"As with every other kind of elite, these mighty beings must say, "I am me. This is my ID and home-root. And yes, I did that."

It is anonymity, after all, that is the transgressor's default evasion of consequences; one can only be held accountable when one can be positively identified.

Making individual AIs identifiable, then, opens up all kinds of possibilities in their governance that might never have occurred to us, let alone explored, before.

We still need to attach a *how* to Brin's proposition. A registration system assigning every AI an ID, plus "an operational-referential kernel", would do the trick (he calls this a "Soul Kernel"). When individual identity in place, it would become possible to incentivize AIs to compete for rewards in the task of "detecting and denouncing those of their peers who behave in ways we deem insalubrious.

"Not only does this approach farm out enforcement to entities who are inherently better capable of detecting and denouncing each other's problems or misdeeds," Brin explains, "the method has another, added advantage. It might continue to function, even as these competing entities get smarter and smarter, long after the regulatory tools used by organic humans - and prescribed now by most AI experts - lose all ability to keep up.

"Putting it differently, if none of us organics can keep up with the programs, then how about we recruit entities who inherently *can* keep up? Because the watchers are made of the same stuff as the watched."

He goes on that in this paradigm, AIs would not be under centralized control, or even overseen by human laws. "Rather, I want these new kinds of über-minds encouraged and empowered to hold each other accountable, the way we already (albeit imperfectly) do. By sniffing at each other's operations and schemes, then motivated to tattle or denounce when they spot bad stuff.

"If the right incentives are in place - say, rewards for whistle-blowing that grant more memory or processing power, or access to physical resources, when some bad thing is stopped - then this kind of accountability rivalry just might keep pace, even as AI entities keep getting smarter and smarter. No bureaucratic agency could keep up at that point. But rivalry among them - tattling by equals - might."

He argues that this would create a balance – the only truly viable on – between positive and negative AI outcomes.

"...perhaps those super-genius programs will realize it is in their own best interest to maintain a competitively accountable system, like the one that made ours the most successful of all human civilizations. One that evades both chaos and the wretched trap of monolithic power by kings or priesthoods... or corporate oligarchs... or Skynet monsters. The only civilization that, after millennia of dismally stupid rule by moronically narrow-minded centralized regimes, finally dispersed creativity and freedom and accountability widely enough to become truly inventive."

It's the most efficient way to get to true AI regulation, he asserts – no artificial moral or ethical imperatives, no idealistic codes, just "the Enlightenment approach - incentivizing the smartest members of civilization to keep an eye on each other, on our behalf.

"I don't know that it will work; it's just the only thing that possibly can."

A New Cognitive Age

The potential for a merger between humanity and AI is so great that its supporters have created a new paradigm for it in the schema of life: the *Seventh Kingdom*, domain of an entirely new form of life.

This new species includes human beings who are augmented with bionic parts, and whose brains detect and process senses beyond the traditional five, and are able to communicate with digital systems. Needless to say, fans of this thinking also expect that our cyborg selves will not only live longer but enjoy a much greater quality of life.

Before we get that far, we note that the merger of human brains and AI brains is already underway, even if they aren't literally plugged into each other.

John Nosta writes in *Psychology Today* that our personal reality is based on our thoughts, and as AI is now also shaping our thoughts, it is therefore helping to shape our reality. Our cognitive potential, he argues, is being redefined by this new conncction, and our future will be a partnership, in a reality that is both human and AI.

"As you think, so you act," he wrote. "As you act, so you become."

That axiom, he wrote, "is gathering fresh momentum in the present-day reality, reshaped by the emerging interfaces of technology, artificial intelligence, and human cognition."

The idea that our thoughts define our reality isn't new. Even the ancient philosophers were onto this truth, and leaders good and evil have leveraged it to shape our social universe through most of civilization. As our thinking changes, so does our internal model of the world; when some other force beyond our own conscious awareness is guiding that change, our internal world is changed in ways that suit our influencer.

The moral philosophy of this truth aside, "Our cognitive landscapes are not only transmuting into AI-powered arenas but are also gradually becoming an inseparable part of them," Nosta wrote. For better or worse, this is happening.

The implications are significant. AI is becoming more than just a tool; it will literally become our cognitive partner, both very personally and in the arena of the global social experience.

On the one hand, AI becomes a powerful component of our individual thought, helping us process information more efficiently, guiding us to higher-quality decision-making, and steering us from error (assuming we use it wisely). On the other, our minds will pull in AI's direction, as we learn to literally create and inhabit new digital realities that leverage our very human brainpower.

"Such technological breakthroughs do not just represent an augmentation of human cognition," he went on. "They are a testament to the paradigm shift in our understanding of the relationship between thought and reality."

There will come a day when the line between the human and the AI in the thought processes of each is blurred beyond definition. That may even happen in our lifetimes. We can only imagine the world that will result.

And for now, we're stepping into a new era, hand-in-hand with AI, that will change the way we live in and experience the world. It will be a change like no other we've ever been through, in all of human history. We will, with AI, become something completely new.

"The dawn of the cognitive age signifies more than a technological revolution," he concluded. "It heralds a redefinition of our relationship with reality, a newfound partnership with AI, and a broader understanding of our cognitive powers. The ripple effects of this cognitive revolution will not only define the present, but they will also shape an extraordinary reality for our future - a future where we will navigate the world not merely as observers but as active, cognitive constructors."

☐

If you enjoyed *The Pod Bay Doors, Vol. II*, please consider sharing your opinion in an Amazon review!

Sources/Recommended Reading

Books

The Age of AI: And Our Human Future, Henry Kissinger, Eric Schmidt, Daniel Huttenlocher. Little, Brown and Company, 2021.

Artificial Intelligence: A Guide for Thinking Humans, Melanie Mitchell. Farrar, Straus and Giroux, 2019.

Godel, Escher, Bach: An Eternal Golden Brain, Douglas Hofstadter. Basic Books, 1979.

I Am a Strange Loop, Douglas Hofstadter. Basic Books, 2007.

Michaelmas, Algis Budrys. Open Road Media, 1977

Articles

Bellaiche, L., et al. (2023) "Humans versus AI: whether and why we prefer human-created compared to AI-created artwork". Cognitive Research: Principles and Implications, vol. 8:42.

Internet sources

https://theconversation.com/ai-is-an-existential-threat-just-not-the-way-you-think-207680

https://www.indy100.com/science-tech/milla-sofia-teen-influencer-ai

https://virtual-idol.fandom.com/wiki/Yuki_Terai

https://www.wired.com/story/give-every-ai-a-soul-or-else/

https://futurism.com/ai-generated-influencers

https://www.psychologytoday.com/ca/blog/the-digital-self/202307/ai-as-cognitive-partner-a-new-cognitive-age-dawns

https://davidbrin.wordpress.com/2023/02/17/the-troubles-begin-when-ai-earns-our-empathy/

https://www.fastcompany.com/90909881/artificial-intelligence-and-the-evolution-of-trust

https://www.gatesnotes.com/The-risks-of-AI-are-real-but-manageable

https://www.technologyreview.com/2023/06/28/1075683/humans-may-be-more-likely-to-believe-disinformation-generated-by-ai/

https://davidbrin.blogspot.com/2023/07/can-dumb-apes-plan-for-future-ai.html

https://www.whitehouse.gov/ostp/ai-bill-of-rights/

https://www.axios.com/pro/tech-policy/2023/04/25/exclusive-progressives-press-biden-to-issue-an-ai-executive-order

https://www.americanprogress.org/article/the-needed-executive-actions-to-address-the-challenges-of-artificial-intelligence/

https://www.pewresearch.org/internet/wp-content/uploads/sites/9/2023/06/PI_2023.06.21_Best-Worst-Digital-Life_2035_FINAL.pdf

https://fortune.com/2023/07/31/why-ai-artificial-intelligence-perfect-psychopath-neuroscientist/

https://www.scientificamerican.com/article/the-computer-scientist-training-ai-to-think-with-analogies/

https://www.forbes.com/sites/cindygordon/2023/07/29/norway-endless-beauty-and-endless-ai-leadership/amp/

https://www.openculture.com/2018/01/artificial-intelligence-writes-a-piece-in-the-style-of-bach.html

https://futurism.com/the-byte/impossible-chatbots-stop-lying-experts

https://thechatbot.net/are-virtual-girlfriends-the-relationship-of-the-future/

https://cmte.ieee.org/futuredirections/2023/05/15/ai-driven-virtual-girlfriend-overstepping-boundaries/

https://www.newsweek.com/artificial-intelligence-ai-girlfriend-chatbot-influencer-1801379

https://www.microsoft.com/en-us/p/kari-virtual-girlfriend/9nblggh6hz23

https://www.thestar.com.my/tech/tech-news/2023/07/16/thousands-chatted-with-this-ai-039virtual-girlfriend039-then-things-got-even-weirder
https://www.popsci.com/technology/ai-beatles-song-john-lennon/

https://futurism.com/the-byte/impossible-chatbots-stop-lying-experts

https://www.theguardian.com/lifeandstyle/2023/may/22/there-was-all-sorts-of-toxic-behaviour-timnit-gebru-on-her-sacking-by-google-ais-dangers-and-big-techs-biases

https://time.com/6132399/timnit-gebru-ai-google/

https://www.technologyreview.com/2023/08/09/1077516/watermarking-ai-trust-online/

https://arstechnica.com/science/2023/07/a-jargon-free-explanation-of-how-ai-large-language-models-work/

https://blog.ap.org/standards-around-generative-ai

https://theconversation.com/3-ways-ai-is-transforming-music-210598

https://www.popsci.com/technology/nvidia-chip-generative-ai/

https://www.publishersweekly.com/pw/by-topic/digital/content-and-e-books/article/92471-ai-is-about-to-turn-book-publishing-upside-down.html

https://futurism.com/studios-ai-replace-background-actors

https://futurism.com/the-byte/fury-chatgpt-replace-writers

https://cointelegraph.com/news/hollywood-studios-reject-banning-ai-from-writer-s-rooms

https://futurism.com/the-byte/michio-kaku-big-problem-artificial-intelligence?fbclid=Iwhttps://futurism.com/the-byte/michio-kaku-big-problem-artificial-intelligence

https://hbr.org/2021/07/quantum-computing-is-coming-what-can-it-do

https://www.zdnet.com/article/quantum-computers-eight-ways-quantum-computing-is-going-to-change-the-world/

https://www.wired.com/story/chatgpt-scams-fraudgpt-wormgpt-crime/

https://www.wired.com/story/labgenius-antibody-factory-machine-learning/dium=email&utm_source=nl&utm_term=P4

https://brand-studio.fortune.com/cognizant/harnessing-the-power-of-generative-AI-to-reimagine-health-care/

https://www.hollywoodreporter.com/business/business-news/ai-works-not-copyrightable-studios-1235570316/

https://www.youtube.com/watch?v=VQNcZyQC6sM

https://futurism.com/the-byte/bill-gates-ai-elections-democracy

https://www.cbsnews.com/news/henry-kissinger-at-100-artificial-intelligence-global-tensions-and-addressing-his-critics/

https://www.bushcenter.org/catalyst/global-challenges/kissinger-on-artificial-intelligence-authoritarianism-hope

https://www.theatlantic.com/magazine/archive/2018/06/henry-kissinger-ai-could-mean-the-end-of-human-history/559124/

https://time.com/6113393/eric-schmidt-henry-kissinger-ai-book/

https://fortune.com/2023/05/08/henry-kissinger-ai-nuclear-weapons-warning-risk/

https://www.economist.com/by-invitation/2023/04/28/yuval-noah-harari-argues-that-ai-has-hacked-the-operating-system-of-human-civilisation

https://www.deepmind.com/blog/rt-2-new-model-translates-vision-and-language-into-action

https://robotics-transformer2.github.io/assets/rt2.pdf

https://time.com/6266923/ai-eliezer-yudkowsky-open-letter-not-enough/

About the Author

Scott Robinson is a technologist, social scientist, public speaker and musician, and serves as Director of Technology and Content for the non-profit Humanity Prime.

He can be found at

scott.robinson@glenmillscience.com

☐ ☐ ☐

www.ingramcontent.com/pod-product-compliance
Lightning Source LLC
Chambersburg PA
CBHW020655220526
45464CB00001B/441